# Nyx
## in the HOUSE of NIGHT

# Other YA Smart Pop Titles

*Demigods and Monsters*
on Rick Riordan's Percy Jackson and the Olympians Series

*A New Dawn*
on Stephenie Meyer's Twilight Series

*Secrets of the Dragon Riders*
on Christopher Paolini's Inheritance Saga

*Mind-Rain*
on Scott Westerfeld's Uglies Series

*Flirtin' with the Monster*
on Ellen Hopkins' *Crank* and *Glass*

*A Visitor's Guide to Mystic Falls*
on *The Vampire Diaries*

*Through the Wardrobe*
on C.S. Lewis' Chronicles of Narnia

*The Girl Who Was on Fire*
on Suzanne Collins' Hunger Games Trilogy

# Nyx
## IN THE
## HOUSE *of* NIGHT

{ MYTHOLOGY, FOLKLORE, AND RELIGION
IN THE P.C. AND KRISTIN CAST
VAMPYRE SERIES }

{ EDITED BY }

## P.C. Cast

with LEAH WILSON
illustrations by ALAN TORRANCE

SMART
POP

AN IMPRINT OF BENBELLA BOOKS, INC. | DALLAS, TEXAS

Smart Pop is an Imprint of BenBella Books, Inc.
10440 North Central Expressway, Suite 800
Dallas, TX 75231
www.benbellabooks.com
www.smartpopbooks.com
Send feedback to feedback@benbellabooks.com

Printed in the United States of America
10 9 8 7 6 5 4 3

Library of Congress Cataloging-in-Publication Data is available for this title.
ISBN 978-1-935618-55-3

Copyediting by Erica Lovett and Olubunmi Mia Olufemi
Proofreading by Michael Fedison
Cover design by Sammy Yuen, Jr.
Text design and composition by Neuwirth & Associates, Inc.
Printed by Versa Press

Distributed by Perseus Distribution
http://www.perseusdistribution.com/

To place orders through Perseus Distribution:
Tel: (800) 343-4499
Fax: (800) 351-5073
E-mail: orderentry@perseusbooks.com

Special discounts for bulk sales (minimum of 25 copies) are available. Please contact Aida Herrera at aida@benbellabooks.com.

# { Contents }

# { Introduction }

P.C. CAST

EVEN BEFORE I hit national bestseller lists, the two questions readers asked me more than any other were: 1) Where do you get your ideas? And 2) How much research do you do?

Okay, the two answers go hand in hand. Research has always been the foundation of my ideas. I actually enjoy researching, and I like doing it old style—paging through giant history and humanities textbooks in a musty research section of a library. As I go through tomes on history and sociology and mythology, my mind starts creating stories and pictures: changing, shifting, modernizing, rewriting. This process has always seemed totally normal to me. Ancient mythological tragedy? Bah! Everyone dies tragically with no happily ever after in history? No way! For as long as I can remember I've revised mythology, created worlds based on history, and then made the stories read the way I wanted them to read—quite often giving unexpected characters happily every afters and turning patriarchy and misogyny upside down.

That's usually how I begin my writing process, with research. But from my very first book I realized that I created better, more believable worlds if I mixed textbook research with legwork. That's one of the reasons so many of my novels are set in Oklahoma. When I describe the Centaur Plains in my fictional world of Partholon, it's really Oklahoma's Tall Grass Prairie. I've been there—walked its paths—gotten lost in its majesty. As I'm there I create worlds of my own and populate them with unusual characters. I tell their stories first in my mind, and then on paper.

Now, enter the House of Night and bestsellerdom. There are lots of awesome things about being a bestselling novelist. Meeting my literary heroes, like Pat Conroy and Sue Monk Kidd, is one big plus (but that's a different kind of essay!). Another plus is that being successful has provided me the means to expand my research legwork. So when I made the Vampyre High Council's headquarters on San Clemente Island just off the coast of Venice, I did so because I'd been there and become enchanted by that tiny island within view of Venice's Saint Mark's Basilica.

I decided to incorporate Capri into the history of the House of Night world, and to make the site of the ancient home of the High Council there, after visiting that fabulous blue island and being mesmerized by its beauty. In the same research trip I walked the streets of Pompeii and knew immediately that I had to add its tragic history into my House of Night mythology, as well.

So you can see that when the fabulous editor Leah Wilson, head of Ben-Bella Books' Smart Pop series, approached me for permission to create a non-fiction anthology based on what was basically the research roots of the House of Night, not only was I excited about the idea—I also wanted to join the group of authors! That's how my essay, "Cruithne Mythology and the House of Night," was born. I loved writing it and being able to show my readers exactly how I weave history and mythology into my own fictional tapestry.

I also loved taking on the role of pseudo-editor (make no mistake, readers, Leah Wilson is the real editor of this collection—I'm just the cheerleader). By playing editor I got to invite some of my favorite people and authors to join our team and chime in with their own perspectives regarding the House of Night's mythology. It was especially fun to put the ex-editor of my Goddess Summoning series, and longtime friend, Christine Zika, in the position of author-to-my-editing by asking her to write for me! And what a great essay she created. Her take on worshipping the female deity was especially cool for me to read, because I've known her for more than a decade and have appreciated her strength and guidance as my personal writing mentor. After all, my nickname for her has long been Goddess Editor!

It was a pleasure to be able to include Bryan Lankford, who is the "real" Dragon Lankford and a well-respected author in his own right. I thoroughly enjoyed his play on being a House of Night professor and I loved the experience and insights into Wicca he brought to this collection, as well as his reflections on how I have lovingly adapted pieces of his belief system within my fictional worship of Nyx.

Jana Oliver, Jeri Smith-Ready, Yasmine Galenorn, and Jordan Dane are longtime author friends of mine. I'm so glad that when I put out the call for House of Night essays they answered with imagination and enthusiasm. Jana's piece on tattoos gets an especially big thumbs-up from me. Not just because tattoos play a major role in the House of Night, but also because I have several pieces of body art myself! Jeri first caught my attention when I read her amazing novel *Requiem for the Devil,* in which she sets up the ultimate freedom-of-choice scenario—glad to see she used that unique insight when she discussed freedom of choice in the House of Night mythos, too. I have long appreciated the strength of Yasmine's dedication to the Divine Feminine, and her essay on the Goddess is both empowering and thought provoking. With Jordan's piece it was great to have a fellow Oklahoman weigh in on the Native American magick that runs through our great state and how I borrow from it to create a foundation for Zoey and Grandma Redbird.

And, of course, I love it when Kristin gets a chance to write something on her own; her insights into the House of Night world and the complexities of giving the ancient matriarchal freedoms—as in Zoey being able to choose more than one boyfriend—voice in a modern world are fascinating. As usual, she makes her mom proud.

Though I don't know Karen Mahoney, John Edgar Browning, Ellen Steiber, Amy Sturgis, or Trinity Faegen, their essays delighted me. Who doesn't want to know more about the Otherworld or the House of Night cats, historical vampires or Nyx herself? And I have to tell you, my favorite of the entire collection might just be Amy's amazing piece on Tulsa. I do heart me some T-Town.

A particular point of pleasure I found in putting together this collection was when BenBella agreed to include illustrations by a good friend of mine, Alan Torrance. I was introduced to Alan when I began my research in Scotland for the seventh House of Night book, *Burned.* I recognized his talent then, and am so pleased to be able to show his unique artistic eye in the exquisite pieces he created for *Nyx in the House of Night.*

I hope you enjoy this collection as much as Leah and I enjoyed putting it together. From the heart of the House of Night, I wish you all the brightest of blessings and the magick of mythology to add to your own personal dreams and wishes and stories!

# { Night in the House of Good and Evil }

## NYX'S PORTRAYAL
## IN THE HOUSE OF NIGHT SERIES

*There also stands the gloomy house of Night;*
*ghastly clouds shroud it in darkness.*
*Before it Atlas stands erect and on his head*
*and unwearying arms firmly supports the broad sky,*
*where Night and Day cross a bronze threshold*
*and then come close and greet each other.*

SO BEGINS the House of Night series, with a quotation taken from Hesiod's *Theogony*. From the very beginning, the reader of P.C. and Kristin Cast's popular series is clued into the fact that Nyx—who is known as Night personified both in the books and in our world's mythology—is at the very center of events. It all comes back to her, as we see time and time again throughout the series.

Nyx, Greek goddess of night, is traditionally known as a primordial god, one of the creators of the world. Before there could be Night—and, therefore, also Day—there was only Chaos, and it was Chaos who conceived a daughter and named her Nyx. In turn, Nyx gave birth to a daughter, Hemera (Day). As we can see from Hesiod's version of events in the epigraph that opens the entire series, Night and Day "come close and greet each other" as they fulfill their designated roles. When you find the full passage from which the extract is taken, however, it becomes clear that the reference is literal,[1] rather than just metaphorical. Nyx does indeed share a "house" (or a cave, in some versions) with Hemera, but they can't spend quality time together. "When one comes home through the back door," Judika Illes says, in her *Encyclopedia of Spirits*, "the other leaves through the front." As Hugh G. Evelyn-White translates it:

> And the house never holds them both within; but always one is without the house passing over the earth, while the other stays at home and waits until the time for her journeying to come.

We haven't yet heard anything significant about Hemera—or Day—in the House of Night series, apart from a slight nod to her in the very first book (right after Zoey is Marked, a dorky kid who witnesses the event runs off "to Mrs. Day's room." I can't help but smile at that pairing of Night and Day on the same page, although Mrs. Day herself isn't significant). But perhaps Day's absence is appropriate considering how the two goddesses must live such separate lives.

As with all mythologies, there are other versions of how Nyx came into being. One of the Orphic myths (writings ascribed to Orpheus) even says that Nyx, rather than being brought forth as the eldest child of Chaos, existed from the *very beginning of time*. She appeared in the guise of a great black-winged bird, hovering eternally in darkness—perhaps as though she were the night sky itself. (I find this image to be remarkably evocative of the Raven Mockers from later books in the series, though those great black-winged "bird men" are creatures of *darkness*, rather than creatures belonging to the personification of Night—a difference we'll be looking at later on.)

We first meet the House of Night series' Nyx in the opening book, *Marked*, when Zoey Redbird (previously Zoey Montgomery) is found in school and

---

[1] Well, as "literal" as anything can truly be when it comes to mythology.

Marked by a Tracker from the House of Night. As is the custom, she is formally greeted and summoned to take her place as a vampyre fledgling with other "trainee" vampyres. It is on these opening pages that we are shown how significant Nyx is—and will become:

> Zoey Montgomery! Night has chosen thee; thy death will be thy birth.
> Night calls to thee; hearken to Her sweet voice. Your destiny awaits you
> at the House of Night!

When Zoey first encounters the Goddess, in one of the most powerful scenes in the opening book, Nyx tells her:

> I have Marked you as my own. You will be my first true Daughter of
> Night in this age . . . Zoey Redbird, Daughter of the Night, I name you
> my eyes and ears in the world today, a world where good and evil are
> struggling to find balance.

The reader is immediately made aware that Zoey is special; she has been set apart as something other, something *more* than just the usual breed of fledgling. She is a *Daughter of Night*, and just as Nyx has had many children according to myth—children who play hugely important roles in the workings of the world—Zoey finds that she, too, will be forced to become a part of events far greater than she could ever have imagined.

Nyx is an interesting choice of goddess for the vampyres to worship; she is firmly rooted in Greek mythology, and yet large parts of the House of Night world-building are influenced by other cultures and religions—in particular Pagan and Wiccan, along with Native American. It's a fascinating mix, especially when Christianity (specifically, Catholicism) is added in the form of the Benedictine nuns led by Sister Mary Angela. In the series Nyx is present in many forms throughout the world—as the Goddess says herself when she tells Zoey: "I am known by many names . . . But you . . . may call me by the name by which your world knows me today, Nyx" (*Marked*). The Greek roots of Nyx are rightly acknowledged, however, when she explains: "In truth, it was the ancient Greeks touched by the Change who first worshipped me as the mother they searched for within their endless Night."

Just as the ancient Greeks worshipped Nyx as a "mother," she is often presented as a mother figure in the series. Some ancient sources also refer to her as "Mother Night" and "kindly Night." There is something profoundly maternal about her during her scenes with Zoey; we see in *Marked* her early appearance as a beautiful Native American woman who makes Zoey feel loved and cared for, though perhaps Zoey sees Nyx in this way because she is on her way to see her Cherokee Grandma when she collapses and has that very first vision. (I think that Nyx is able to change her form according to who she happens to be dealing with; or perhaps, more correctly, her appearance changes only in the *perception* of the mortals blessed enough to lay eyes on her. The Goddess is a chameleon, of sorts, which seems somehow fitting for the personification of night's swift-changing landscape.)

We are also shown a glimpse of a somewhat less compassionate Goddess later on during the ancient scenes where we witness, alongside Zoey, Nyx deal harshly with Kalona. It is certainly true that all deities can be as terrible as they can be kindly; in Homer's *Iliad*, it is revealed that Zeus himself is afraid of angering Nyx. Perhaps it is fair to say that Nyx—whether the night goddess presented in mythology or the version we see in the House of Night books—is, in some ways, no different from the mothers many of us know and love. There's no rule that says being a mother automatically makes you soft and nurturing or, in more general terms, "good." Most people simply do the best they can in a very difficult role: motherhood is one of the toughest jobs out there! Add in the responsibilities of a goddess, and it's no wonder Nyx doesn't always seem as "nice" as we might like her to be. Take, for example, her treatment of Aphrodite, which could definitely be interpreted as a form of "tough love." It might not have been nice, but it did seem effective, and Aphrodite was better off for it.

As one of the great maternal forces in the world of mythology, Nyx had many children. The Children of Nyx—also the name sometimes given to fledglings and vampyres at the House of Night—are well documented in any number of common sources. Putting together the information noted by Hesiod, Homer, and others, Nyx seems to have had as many as twenty. Not all of them are as innocuous as Day, however. Love, Friendship, and Gaiety are among her offspring, but so are Misery, Retribution, and Deceit. It's a fascinating contrast, and one that is thoroughly explored throughout the House of Night series. I don't mean literally, as we don't meet these "actual" children of the mythological

Nyx. But certainly through the trials that Zoey and her friends have to face we see plenty of love and friendship, retribution and deceit. And when in *Marked* Nyx speaks to Zoey of the uncertain morals of the world she is about to enter, I can't help but think of the paradoxical nature of the children Nyx has brought forth. Just as one goddess can give birth to both Misery and Love, so each of the characters carry these same potential polarities within them.

Nyx is described by philosophers and poets (e.g., by Aeschylus) as wearing a dark robe covered in stars—a robe that I imagine would look much like the beautiful black dress covered in metallic silver stars that Erik Night gives Zoey for her first ritual as leader of the Dark Daughters in *Betrayed*. In ancient Greek art, Nyx is often depicted as travelling across the sky in a horse-drawn carriage, which could explain Zoey's and the House of Night's connection to horses.

In Greek mythology, the goddess Nyx is quite naturally allied with images of the night sky—especially those focused on the moon and stars. This is reflected in the House of Night series in a number of ways: for example, the sapphire-blue crescent moon that appears on each vampyre fledgling's forehead to show that he or she has been Marked. In *Hunted*, after the battle is won (at least temporarily), we are left with the following scene: "The clouds had completely dissipated, leaving the sky clear to expose a brilliant crescent moon that shone so bright it burned away any lingering confusion and sadness." Imagery of the moon—especially the crescent moon—is often used in the House of Night books and provides a powerful visual symbol. Readers are never allowed to forget *who* is ever-present throughout the dark and often deadly events of these books.

Speaking of "dark" events, the concept of "darkness" in the House of Night series is a complicated one. The word itself can refer to literal darkness or the metaphorical kind—evil. And as Nyx tells Zoey way back in *Marked*: "Darkness does not always equate to evil, just as light does not always bring good." Sister Mary Angela echoes this idea during the final battle in *Hunted*, when she senses the very real (metaphorical) darkness radiating from Neferet. The fallen High Priestess is quick to remind the nun: "Of course you sense darkness from me. My Goddess is Night personified!" To which Sister Mary Angela calmly replies, "No, I am acquainted with Nyx, and though she personifies Night, she doesn't traffic with darkness." Think, too, of the black and white bulls used in later House of Night books to represent the ultimate battle between Light and Darkness (Light is represented by the *black* bull, and Darkness by the white). In the House of Night series, things are not always what they seem.

Darkness is present in the House of Night series in yet another way: Erebus, the Greek personification of Darkness. It is Erebus who is the significant "other" in the Goddess' life—not, as I might originally have expected, Nyx's daughter, Day. Though he has yet to appear in the series (despite Neferet's bogus claims that Kalona is Erebus reborn), he casts a shadowy presence over the characters' lives. Zoey first learns of Erebus during her introductory classes at the House of Night when Neferet teaches her students that "Nyx has a consort, the god Erebus, to whom she is devoted." These words come back to haunt Zoey and her friends later on, when Neferet tries to convince the vampyres that Kalona— the fallen immortal—is really Erebus returned to the world.

Erebus also makes an indirect appearance in the series through a group called the Sons of Erebus, whom me meet in the third book, *Chosen*. These are fierce vampyre warriors sworn to protect the House of Night and all within its walls. They dress entirely in black and are deeply devoted to Nyx, and through the character of Darius—who later becomes Aphrodite's personal Warrior and protector—we learn just how loyal the Sons can be. When he meets Zoey, he says: "The Sons of Erebus will protect Nyx's school with our last breath." This is spoken as simple fact but becomes more of a prophecy later on, when some of the Sons of Erebus die trying to protect the House from Kalona and Neferet.

Much of the mythology surrounding Nyx and Erebus (or Erebos, as he is sometimes known) is sketchy, at best. You have to dig a little deeper and read tales of other gods and goddesses in order to glean any useful information. Most of the stories recount that Nyx and Erebus were brother and sister—both born of Chaos, with Nyx as the elder of the two—and yet Erebus was also Nyx's faithful consort, bringing many of her children into the world with her, including (according to Hesiod's *Theogony*) Day and Light. It seems particularly symbolic that the deities representing Night and Darkness should bring Day and Light into the world; this seeming paradox holds the seed of much of the dramatic tension in myths and folklore throughout the world—and this duality is certainly exploited in the House of Night series.

Erebus' absence from the series makes him an appropriately shadowy figure in another way. Some versions of his story say he is the God of Shadow, rather than simply the God of Darkness, lending him a slightly more sinister feel. He may even have resided in the Underworld—the land of the dead. But regardless of his roots, he is yet another thing that allows us to see the true power of Nyx as presented in the Casts' world: the Goddess' consort is relegated to the sidelines. No matter how many mentions or minor appearances there might be of other gods and goddesses, the House of Night series seems to have only one major deity.

Of course, Greek mythology is not the only place we should look for material that might inform our understanding of a figure as mysterious and complex as Nyx. As the Goddess says herself, in *Marked*: "I am known by many names . . . Changing Woman, Gaea, A'akuluujjusi, Kuan Yin, Grandmother Spider, and even Dawn." Although many of these goddesses are more accurately described as earth goddesses—Gaea being the most obvious and perhaps most well-known example—there is a genuine link between the nature of such deities and Nyx herself. Changing Woman is the Navajo goddess of the changing seasons, and some stories even say she created earth and sky (whereas others say she was the *child* of earth and sky). She is a benevolent figure and one deeply invested in the health and happiness of her people— just as Nyx herself is in the House of Night books.

Kuan-Yin (or Guanyin) is a primarily East Asian Buddhist deity, sometimes known as the goddess of mercy and compassion and called simply "Kannon" in Japan. What is especially interesting about her is that some scholars believe she is associated with the Virgin Mary—an idea that comes up in the House of Night series when Sister Mary Angela voices her belief that Mary and Nyx are different faces of the same deity. In seventeenth-century Japan, Christianity was banned and it became necessary for believers to follow their faith in secret. Some groups managed to continue their worship of the Virgin Mary by using statues disguised as the goddess Kannon. In *Tempted*, Damien even mentions this practice in reference to the spread of Christianity throughout Europe:

> You should remember that in your *Fledgling Handbook 101*, Mary is illustrated as one of the many faces of Nyx . . . It is well documented that during the influx of Christianity into Europe, shrines to Gaea, as well as Nyx, were converted to shrines for Mary long before people converted to the new [religion].

Grandmother Spider, also mentioned by Nyx in the first House of Night novel, created the world in many Native American legends. In some references she seems more like an earth goddess, but in others she is seen as the creator of the stars in the sky. Her web is the sky itself, and drops of dew caught on each silken strand are the stars.

There are many other instances of night goddesses in world mythology that Nyx does not mention, like Hine-Nui-te-pō, the Māori goddess of night, whose name is usually translated as "Great Lady of the Night." Some online sources refer to her as the goddess of death and ruler of the underworld, as well. She also gave the sunset its red color. It was this final point that made me realize how good a representation of Nyx she would be for the red fledglings led by Stevie Rae—especially with their ability to survive death and their desire to live underground. Even if the Casts didn't consciously borrow from Māori mythology, there is still a sense of *rightness* to those red fledglings as a new "breed" of vampyre among Nyx's people.

In Norse mythology, Night is personified by the goddess Nótt. Stories of this night goddess can apparently be found in the famous *Prose Edda*, one of the primary sources of Norse mythology. It is widely believed to have been written in the thirteenth century by Snorri Sturluson in Iceland and was probably the first time that the history of the various gods and goddesses were given order and written in a coherent form. In it, Nótt gives birth to the personification of Earth, a connection that echoes throughout the House of Night books: all five elements are important to Nyx, but Earth seems to have a special place for her. Again, my mind focuses on Stevie Rae and her affinity for Earth. After all, why would Nyx give the leader of this new breed of vampyres such a strong connection to Earth if it weren't important to her? Mythologically, the Casts associate Nyx with earth goddesses such as Gaea and Changing Woman, not just other goddesses of the night.

Egyptian mythology has a goddess of the sky, Nut. Her name (sometimes spelled *Nuit*) literally translates as "Night," and she is one of the most ancient of all the Egyptian goddesses. It is generally understood that she was originally known as the goddess of the *nighttime sky*, which makes her a reasonable counterpart to Nyx. It's interesting—if not necessarily significant—that the ancient Egyptians often depicted Nut as a sacred cow, and some of the artwork is strangely reminiscent of the black bull and the white bull (representing Light/Dark and good/evil) we learn of in *Burned*.

In the House of Night series, Nyx is also associated with animals, whether it is horses (fledglings take riding lessons and horses are well cared for at the school); the cats that fill the corridors of the House of Night and become bonded to particular students; or more traditionally feared and hated creatures, such as snakes. In book two, *Betrayed*, Zoey says:

> Correct me if I'm wrong, Damien, but aren't snakes closely allied with Nyx? Haven't they gotten a bad reputation because historically they've been symbols of female power, and men wanted to take that power away from women and make it something disgusting and scary instead?

This is a common thread woven throughout the books: myths are re*cast* (pun intended!) to show us that where women have previously been maligned, the "truth" might be somewhat different. In *Betrayed*, Zoey also learns that the Gorgon wasn't a monster who turned men to stone out of hatred, but was in fact a famous vampyre High Priestess whose Goddess-given gift was an affinity for earth. And in *Marked*, it is revealed that the Amazons weren't man-haters at all, but simply powerful female vampyre warriors. (We get even more information on Amazon society in *The Fledgling Handbook 101*.) Being matriarchal—and, by association, pro-female—doesn't automatically mean that a culture has to be anti-men. Although vampyre society is matriarchal, male vampyres are not treated as second-class citizens. As Neferet says in the very first book, "We respect and appreciate the Sons of Night, and consider them our protectors and consorts." Erik Night (and with that last name it was obvious that the talented young actor would become a significant figure in Zoey's life), along with the other male vampyres in the series, is treated with a great deal of admiration (at least until he started acting like a jealous stalker with anger management issues)—and not just for his good looks.

In *Tempted*, this theme of respect and appreciation for each others' differences comes to fruition when Lenobia tells Stevie Rae: "Nyx is *our* Goddess. You can't really believe there is only one deity for a world as complex as ours." This beautifully sums up one way that world mythologies can comfortably coincide. There are as many different belief systems as there are cultures, and despite what some people might think, believing in one doesn't mean you have to discount the rest. This is particularly well demonstrated in the House of Night during *Untamed* when, as I mentioned earlier, Sister Mary Angela tells Zoey: "Child, what I believe is that your Nyx is just another incarnation of our Blessed Mother, Mary."

Which brings us to the most important recasting P.C. and Kristin perform: that of Nyx herself. In mythology and culture, there don't seem to be any major "cults" associated with Nyx (such as the "Cult of Demeter" in Greece or the "Cult of Isis" in Egypt), nor are there specific stories written down by the classical scholars and philosophers devoted *entirely* to her. She appears, instead, in more of a supporting role during other tales, standing in the wings—or the shadows—pushing her many children to center stage. By choosing Nyx as their vampyre Goddess, the Casts did something entirely smart: they chose a goddess with a relatively "clean slate" upon which to build their *own* mythology. The result is a truly rich and fascinating world, and I look forward to seeing where the House of Night's incarnation of Nyx takes us next.

KAREN MAHONEY has been published alongside some of her favorite authors in paranormal anthologies like *The Eternal Kiss* (2009) and *Kiss Me Deadly* (2010). She is still in complete shock about this. Her YA novel about alchemy and dark elves, *The Iron Witch*, was published by Flux in the United States and is available now. She is British, but hopes that you do not hold this against her. Please visit her at www.kazmahoney.com.

# { The Dangerous Dead }

## VAMPIRE MYTHOLOGY
## IN THE HOUSE OF NIGHT SERIES

*John Edgar Browning*

READING THE House of Night series is very much akin to reading Zoey's favorite book, *Dracula* (1897), for like Bram Stoker's novel, one will find also in the House of Night's pages the subtle mingling of folklore and reality with popular fiction. It will probably come as little surprise to readers out there to learn that, when it comes to its vampyres, the House of Night is steeped in all three. However, which parts are "fiction" and which are "reality" may come as a shock and, in some cases, may even seem implausible.

Folklore has almost as many variations on the vampire as there are vampire films (at least 700 of which, or more, belong to Dracula or his semblance alone[1]), and more often than not the two are confused for one another. The House of Night series, and the various associations it conjures up, is no exception to this. However, the series' treatment of the vampire mythology is

---

[1] See John Edgar Browning and Caroline Joan (Kay) Picart, *Dracula in Visual Media: Film, Television, Comic Book, and Video Game Appearances* (2011).

surprisingly faithful to the folklore, a rarity among vampire fiction, which often relies too heavily on screen vampires. This is not to say that the series does not also draw from popular film and TV presentations; it does. And together we shall unearth the House of Night's mythological foundation, in an attempt to separate fact and fiction from myth and folklore.

Before continuing any further, however, I would like first to discern, for the sake of clarity, what is meant by the four variations of the word "vampire" readers will come across in this chapter. When speaking of the undead in the House of Night, I shall use the term (1) *vampyre*, in keeping with the series' spelling. Thus, the more familiar spelling with (2) *vampire* shall be reserved for filmic and other literary representations of the undead. If I wish to refer to the undead in whom, for centuries, central and eastern European villagers have believed (and in some places still do believe), I shall use the term (3) *revenant*. And when, in the latter part of this chapter, I refer to real, walking, talking, self-identifying human vampires, I shall use for them the term (4) *vampi(y)re*.

## THE REVENANT OF FOLKLORE

To begin our analysis of the House of Night, let us consider first the series' wider use of the more traditional elements of myth and folklore. By this is meant what the good Reverend Montague Summers, a noted scholar of the occult, aptly termed "vampirism proper."[2] A consideration of these areas now will be particularly beneficial later on when we begin mapping out the House of Night series' occasional use of the trendier vampire conventions.

Now, the first errand in our quest to unearth the vampire myth in the House of Night shall take us 300 years into the past to find the European "revenant." The revenant, the "dangerous dead"[3] of folklore, was not just a vampire in the modern sense of the term. Rather, he scarcely resembled his counterpart on-screen, according to noted folklorist Dr. Paul Barber.[4] This

---

[2] Montague Summers, *The Vampire: His Kith and Kin* (1928).
[3] The "dangerous dead" is a phrase Paul Barber uses frequently in his seminal work, *Vampires, Burial, and Death: Folklore and Reality* (1988), to describe those who have died then afterwards returned, or will likely return, from the grave to do harm on the living.
[4] Barber, *Vampires, Burial, and Death.*

malevolent figure, whose physical attributes we'll review momentarily, was to central and eastern European villagers of centuries past the ghost of a recently deceased relative or neighbor. He or she would visit them in their bedchambers at night and take from them their blood or energy, or, more simply, their vital essence. Such an attack meant either a sudden or lingering death for the villager and the likelihood of returning from the grave as a revenant, as well.

In hindsight, it's interesting to note that the revenant's handiwork was never actually detected by the villagers until after the death of the second or third victim, who usually reported having seen, before his or her untimely demise, the ghostly figure of the villager who had died initially. Fearful villagers would then proceed *en masse* to the grave of the first villager, whom by that point they suspected of being the revenant causing all the mayhem. There they would observe the traditional custom of exhuming (or digging up) the villager's body, usually after it had lain in the earth for some weeks.

Unfortunately, the villagers' knowledge of decompositional processes was quite limited. As a result, the macabre scene they uncovered was to those present nothing short of proof-positive that the deceased had issued forth from the grave and attacked the living. The "signs" they would have taken for evidence, briefly sketched: The body might have appeared fresh and undecomposed, and without the presence of odor[5] that was generally thought characteristic of the dead (though not everywhere, as we'll discuss shortly in reference to Stevie Rae and the other dead fledglings). The body might have seemed in appearance quite plump (i.e., as though well fed), and its position in the grave might have been altered. Its limbs would very likely have been pliable rather than stiff, and its mouth, which before burial had been securely shut (so as to prevent entry by malevolent spirits), might have been open, as would one or both eyes (which, like the corpse's mouth, had been closed also before burial). The face might have appeared ruddy (or red) and fresh; "fresh"

---

[5] Barber observes in *Vampires, Burial, and Death* that the signification of "odor" is not, in the folklore of the revenant, regionally consistent throughout Europe. For example, villagers living in geographically cooler areas (where, unbeknownst to them, cooler soil acted more or less as a preserving agent) naturally concluded that the "unnatural" *absence* of odor was indicative of vampirism. On the other hand, the *presence* of odor was interpreted much in the same way by villagers living in geographically warmer areas.

blood (i.e., someone else's blood) might have appeared around the mouth, nose, eyes, and ears, and the shirt or death shroud might have laid partially or completely soaked in "fresh" blood. The chin and face might have revealed a freshly grown stubble, and hair elsewhere might also appear to have grown after death. The nails, too, might appear longer or else might appear to have fallen away, revealing in their place "freshly" grown ones.

Convinced that before them lay a revenant, the villagers would then proceed to kill the corpse a "second time" using whatever means was at their disposal. One such method involved piercing the heart with an actual wooden stake (a method we see used often on modern vampires). As final proof for their actions, the villagers, upon staking the suspected revenant, might have witnessed the corpse let out an audible groan, or "death cry," while secreting simultaneously more "fresh" blood from its orifices. Most puzzling of all, the corpse—if male—might have experienced an erection, right there on the spot. If the corpse had been female, the vulva might have looked in appearance, to those present at the gravesite, both swollen and discolored.[6]

Of course, nowadays we are more knowledgeable about such things and understand them to be normal postmortem processes. Nonetheless, what I find particularly striking here, in the interests of this chapter, is the apparent overlap between the House of Night series and the documented cases of village revenants. For example, we know that, in the House of Night, the hair and nails of fledgling vampyres grow exceptionally fast during the "Change." In fact, they grow so fast that "after a little practice," Zoey notes in *Betrayed*, "you can tell what year a fledgling is without checking the crest on her jacket."

So what about fangs, readers may well be asking? After all, fewer fangs in the movies generally meant that viewers could also expect less blood . . . and sex, since all three are often tied together metaphorically. In the case of the House of Night series, the adult and fledgling vampyres, with the exception of postmortem Stevie Rae and the other "red" fledglings, are, well, fangless, to be perfectly blunt. But that doesn't mean they're impotent or castrated. A

---

[6] For further discussion on the numerous ways in which to identify and dispose of a revenant, including the "wild signs" produced by the male and female sex organs discussed in detail in regard to the historical case of Peter Plogojowitz, see Barber's *Vampires, Burial, and Death*.

fledgling's journey into vampyre adulthood carries with it also the growing need to drink blood. More crucially, the blood-exchange ritual between adult vampyres extends decidedly beyond mere sexual metaphor. However, readers may be surprised to learn that while the vampire's tendency to engage in erotic behavior may have prospered in the cinema (as we'll see shortly), by no stretch of the imagination did it start there.

Actually, it was the revenant of folklore who, despite his awful looks, was known to possess a voracious sexual appetite. What's more, he didn't even have (or need) fangs to earn his sordid reputation. As Barber points out, historical accounts of vampirism seldom mention the growth of teeth on exhumed bodies, and with good reason, for the teeth of the suspected revenant were generally quite normal-looking, I'm sad to say.[7] Again, with the exception of Stevie Rae and her dead comrades, here is another of the striking similarities between the vampyres in the House of Night series and the folkloric revenant.

Instead, the fang-deprived revenant earned his reputation for promiscuity (postmortem erections aside) because often he went first for his own widow, whom "he [was] apt to wear out . . . with his attentions," as Barber so elegantly puts it.[8] Hence, we may observe here the original necessity for black mourning cloths at funerals, especially the mourning veil worn by the widow, whose identity might thus be shielded from her late husband's subsequent "advances."[9]

Let us turn our attention now to Stevie Rae. I have remarked previously that she and the other red fledgling vampyre creatures demonstrate some of the physical "signs" observed in the exhumed bodies of suspected revenants in eastern and central Europe. Along a similar line, it is equally telling that at the time of and in the days just prior to the death of the vampyre fledglings who don't survive the "Change," various other outward "signs" are given. This time around, however, the "signs" to which I refer are distinctly American. That's right—I said *American.* These physical "signs" or symptoms seem to draw their origin not from continental Europe, but rather from historical accounts of vampirism based out of New England.

---

[7] Barber, *Vampires, Burial, and Death.*
[8] Ibid.
[9] For further discussion, see Barber, *Vampires, Burial, and Death.*

## Real World Red Fledglings

Believe it or not, red fledglings have been around for centuries; the color "red," Barber notes, has long been thought to predispose the living to a life after the grave. In Romania, for example, a child born with red hair and blue eyes, or a "red caul" or amniotic membrane (which is normally, in appearance, a clear or grayish-white) covering its head, was more likely to become a vampire. In the Kashubia region of Poland, red birthmarks indicated the same, as did ruddy (or "red") cheeks and complexions—especially among alcoholics, whose tendency to turn red in the face indicated to local villagers at the time the "sinfulness" of excessive drinking.

Like their brethren across the Atlantic, New Englanders also believed in the revenant, and like the Europeans they, too, took similar precautionary measures to protect themselves against the "dangerous dead," including exhumations. In the first two installments of the House of Night series, for example, readers may recall the persistent cough, pallor, and rapid wasting away that occur just before a fledging vampyre dies. These outward symptoms mirror the same cough and deteriorative health New Englanders would have observed in (what they believed were) dying revenant victims.

The invisible scourge inflicting these unfortunate New Englanders was most likely pulmonary tuberculosis (TB), known then as "consumption." On the subject of New England vampirism, folklorist Dr. Michael E. Bell notes that the symptoms of TB have many parallels to vampire folklore. For example, New Englanders dying of consumption, according to Bell, suffer mostly at night; they experience an unrelenting cough and severe chest pain (described sometimes as a heavy weight upon the chest); color, strength, and appetite quickly diminish, as well; and worse yet, the cough begins to produce a mucus discharge, or "sputum," that with time grows to become quite thick and bloodied; followed then by bodily emaciation. "A consumptive's appearance," Bell concludes, "ties him to death—and to the vampire."[10]

---

[10] Michael E. Bell, *Food for the Dead: On the Trail of New England's Vampires* (2001).

Bell's description of the physical effects of consumption on the body is reflected as early as the first few chapters of *Marked*. For example, readers may recall the manner in which Zoey describes her physical state after being Marked and beginning the physical Change to vampire. Zoey notes in *Marked*: "I was snotting. I don't mean just sniffling a little. I mean I was wiping my nose on the sleeve of my hoodie (gross). I couldn't breathe without opening my mouth, which made me cough more, and I couldn't believe how badly my chest hurt!" It is interesting, too, that Bell's description surfaces again in Stevie Rae's and Elliot's final moments in *Betrayed* (i.e., the coughing up of blood). Until finally, at the point of death, "blood trickled down from her [Stevie Rae's] mouth, her eyes, nose, and ears," a scene that, looking back to an earlier discussion of ours, is eerily reminiscent of what villagers observed in European burial exhumations.

While we're on the subject of European folklore again, let us take a moment to note the characteristic way in which the dead fledgling vampyres are seen wandering about, generally on or close to the night following their deaths. Curiously, these scenes mirror quite closely the "eyewitness" accounts of the European revenant, whose behavior is similarly described in surviving documentation. But while this particular behavior in the House of Night series is explained easily enough *vis-à-vis* the historically documented cases of European revenants, Stevie Rae and the other red fledglings' lack of a soul does not have so simple, or consistent, an antecedent.

Because beliefs about revenants and souls in folklore have varied greatly according to geography and culture, their full survey here would require far lengthier an explanation than space will allow. However, one avenue to consider briefly is that some European villagers believed that more than one kind of soul occupied the human body simultaneously, and that one of these souls, the "less human" side, stayed behind following death in order to facilitate the decomposition of the body. This, of course, is but one interpretation of the "soul dilemma" in vampire mythology, and if readers dig a little deeper, they're likely to find a cache of bizarre explanations. In brief, some cultures believed, for example, that a malevolent spirit-turned-squatter had commandeered, as it were, the empty space that the villager's departed soul had previously occupied in a sort of postmortem demonic possession. Still others believed that it was actually the deceased's very own soul (in corrupt form) that occupied the body after death, refusing to go to the afterworld because of an untimely demise like suicide, murder, or accidental death, though a sinful life—even alcoholism—could just as easily have been the culprit.

Another quality we observe in Stevie Rae and the red fledglings is a foul smell or offensive body odor, which seems to be a variation on the beliefs surrounding odor and vampirism in folklore (though we later learn that much of the issue with the red fledglings had been due to a lack of showering). During the decompositional process, a foul, gaseous odor is produced by the body, and as I remarked previously, the presence of odor in a corpse was representative of vampirism to villagers in geographically warmer areas. In those days, it was believed that foul odors literally brought with them contagion or plague, similar in nature to the way in which many of us today believe a cold draft can carry illness. Villagers resorted to using garlic, most notably, but also perfumes or other such pungent-smelling substances as a defensive measure to ward off (though in truth they only masked) such threats.[11]

## A Clove of Garlic a Day Keeps the Vampire Away

Some scholars have argued that you can see these beliefs about odor's ability to carry disease, and the protection afforded by sweeter smells, in a popular children's nursery rhyme from the eighteenth century: "Ring around the rosy / Pocket full of *posies*." [italics mine] The "posie," or "nosegay" (literally to keep the nose "gay" or "happy"), is a bouquet of flowers that has for centuries been used for its fragrant quality. So, there could not have been a more useful charm for protecting oneself against the Black Death,[12] as this children's playful rendition of the *danse macabre* (French) or *totentanz* (German) suggests.

---

[11] See Barber's discussion of "apotropaics" and odor.
[12] Randy Page, Galen E. Cole, and Thomas C. Timmreck, *Basic Epidemiological Methods and Biostatistics, A Practical Guidebook* (1995).

I wish to conclude our discussion of the House of Night series' folkloric ancestry by referencing briefly two other motifs of interest in the series: cats and tattoos. Cats, which are discussed at length elsewhere in this book, have shared in their history various superstitions and connections to otherworldly beings, most recognizably the witch. However, readers may be surprised to discover that the cat and the revenant go back a very long way, as well. Hence, it becomes clearer why in various places throughout Europe cats were—and in some cases still are—kept away from dead bodies. This unlikely connection between the witch and the revenant may at first seem unrelated, but these two outcasts have not always been seen as separate species, as Barber and others have been keen to point out.[13]

Finally, there are the striking tattoos that adorn fledgling and adult vampyres. This, admittedly, I found rather perplexing at first, until quite suddenly it struck me that revenants, too, share an odd connection with strange, un/natural marks. In the House of Night, of course, the tattoos serve to "mark" those who are becoming vampyres, and they become more intricate on those who have survived the Change and become full-fledged adult vampyres. Similarly, "marks" of a sort (e.g., ordinary birthmarks, a pronounced mole, a birth defect, etc.) were to European villagers of centuries past a "sign" that the bearer would more than likely survive the grave. The bearers of strange marks in the House of Night have, in effect, survived a death, as well—that of their human selves.

## THE VAMPIRE OF "POPULAR" MYTH

Let us consider now the series' "nuts and bolts" as it were: the more popular variety of conventions one has come to expect—even depend on—in the vampire genre. In fact, it might even be said that without these conventions, the vampire would seem less real, like seeing a ghost in a shopping mall as opposed to a run-down old house. They are what make the vampyres of the House of Night series recognizable as vampires.

Readers will likely remember, in the initial chapters of *Marked* for example, the foreboding, "Gothic" atmosphere in which Zoey finds herself as she

---

[13] Barber, *Vampires, Burial, and Death.*

explores, for the first time, the grounds of the House of Night school. After all, the entire place is, to Zoey, "like something out of a creepy dream": for hung overhead against the night is a "brilliant moon shining above the big old oaks," while the main building, "red brick and black rock" in aspect, is a presence not to be taken lightly at "three stories tall . . . [with] a weirdly high roof that pointed up and then flattened off at the top." The main building is further highlighted by a round tower, which adds to "the illusion that the place [is] much more castle-like than school-like." At this, Zoey begins to wonder whether "a moat would have looked more like it belonged there."

This is a familiar scene to fans of the vampire genre, but contrary to popular belief the mythical revenant or vampire who haunted folklore didn't usually do so from the safety of a scary castle or tower. Nor, I'm afraid, did he or she take a fancy to gnarly trees, owls, bats, or full moons any more than the next ghoul. Such is the product of Gothic literature, whose accepted conventions we have learned over time to recognize and associate with monstrous and deviant representations. As David Pirie remarks in his seminal work *The Vampire Cinema*: "If there is one magic ingredient of the vampire genre in literature or in the cinema, one that sometimes even supersedes the vampire himself, it is the *landscape* he inhabits."[14] Pirie goes on to say that although the vampire may be the one actively scaring us in a film or books, the implied terror—the scary "window dressing," as it were—is the landscape itself. This component of horror stories, he adds, must be present in order to separate the vampire physically and figuratively from what is considered normal and acceptable by society.

The literary and screen vampire is, at its core, an invention of the Gothic movement after all, and its relationship with Gothic landscape and mood is therefore intimately linked. It's worth noting, however, that geographical "remoteness" is a quality shared literally and figuratively by the village revenant, as well. It's perhaps unfortunate then that the revenant could not also share in the same lavish furnishings at home as enjoyed by the more conventional representations of vampires on-screen and in literature. In this respect, the House of Night is no different than its fictional predecessors. Who wouldn't want to go to a Gothic-style boarding school whose students must divide their time between fencing, horseback riding, and flat-screen televisions?

---

[14] David Pirie, *The Vampire Cinema* (1977).

Another aspect in which the vampyres in the House of Night resemble the conventional vampires is in their dashing good looks, and again, we are dealing here with fiction, not folklore. As I explained earlier, the revenant of folklore is the sort one doesn't take home to mother. Instead, it was John Polidori who gave us, in his short story "The Vampyre" (1819), the first "modern" literary vampire, which he based in part on a shorter unpublished piece by Lord Byron (for whom Polidori had worked previously as a traveling physician). Polidori's vampire, the young and handsome Lord Ruthven, transformed the corpselike revenant that had for centuries dominated European folklore into the drop-dead gorgeous vampire that has subsequently dominated literature, film, and television.

Another area worth consideration—one in which the House of Night vampyres break with convention—is their uncommon method of blood-drinking. Readers will undoubtedly recall the peculiar way in which Zoey's tongue, when drinking from Heath in *Betrayed*, "flicked out and licked the blood from his neck." This unusual scene stands noticeably at contrast with the neck-biting and blood-sucking commonly seen in film. Perhaps this is because the House of Night vampyres' blood-drinking roots seem to come not from literature but from the biology of vampire bats. This particular species of bat uses its enlarged canines to mark delicately in the skin a small incision. Afterwards, the blood flows freely from the wound as a result of an anticoagulant in the bat's saliva. Using its specially designed tongue to draw out the blood, the bat then laps it up, as a cat laps up milk.[15]

The exact origin of the endorphins contained in the vampyres' saliva in the House of Night series, on the other hand, is probably related in some way to human sexuality and the pleasure centers of the brain. However, with respect to screen vampires, this particular ability of Zoey's and the adult vampyres' saliva is, it would appear, a sort of naturalization or re-imagining (albeit a more practical one) of the erotic display between vampire and victim that started to develop on-screen in the late 1950s, after America relinquished to the United Kingdom at that time its monopoly on vampire films in general

---

[15] For a full scientific account of this process, see: Christine Hawkey, "Plasminogen Activator in the Saliva of the Vampire Bat Desmodus Rotundus," *Nature* (1966); and Terence Cartwright, "The Plasminogen Activator of Vampire Bat Saliva," *Blood* (1974).

and Dracula films in particular. (The next major American Dracula film would not be released until the late 1970s.) From this point forward in film and literary history, it became customary for the vampire's attack to elicit from victims a more sexualized response. Put simply, though the figure of the vampire itself has been sexualized since its folkloric origins, the victim's conscious, unreserved embrace of the vampire's attack, as in the case of Heath and Zoey, is the invention of film, not folklore.[16]

## Creature Feature

Before the 1950s, vampires frequently wore cloaks or capes in the cinema, a visual cue that figures in the House of Night as well in the markedly Gothic appearance of the red fledglings, who also wear dark cloaks, in *Betrayed*. In keeping with production codes at the time, stage and film producers used capes to obscure or censor from viewers the perceivably erotic and sexualized act of vampiric penetration and blood (or fluid) exchange. Thus, the cape, too, has no origin in folklore, deriving instead from the first stage adaptations of *Dracula* during the mid to late 1920s. Afterwards, this rather useful garment in Dracula's wardrobe carries over into film with Universal's *Dracula* (1931), where it and several other motifs help to cement the image that has been associated with Dracula and vampires ever since.

## VAMPI(Y)RES TODAY

The profound nature of this final section, as readers will soon learn, is one in which I take especial interest. For over a year now, I have visited, with considerable regularity and enthusiasm, the French Quarter and adjacent areas in New Orleans, Louisiana, and conducted there an ethnographic study. In that time, I have discovered that living amongst the Crescent City are perhaps several dozen extraordinary citizens who, quite vehemently, self-identify as

---

[16] A particularly strong example here is Hammer's *Dracula* (United Kingdom, 1958), released as *Horror of Dracula* in the United States.

"vampi(y)re." By this is meant people who consume, or absorb, either human and/or animal blood (sanguinarian), psychic energy (psi-vamp), or both (hybrid), and do so out of a need that they claim derives from the lack of natural energy their bodies produce.

My research in this particular field is ongoing, but some of what I've learned is reflected, in various ways, in the title given to this section. The title's significance is twofold. First, the term "vampi(y)re" is a culmination of the two spellings that remain in regular use today within the community, and it is in the usage of this hybrid term that we may see exemplified the aims of the Voices of the Vampire Community (VVC). The organization's members represent various associated vampi(y)ric "groups, Houses, Orders, paths, beliefs, and segments of the vampi(y)re community who meet and are able to put aside personal differences to work together to discuss, suggest, implement, and support projects, ideas, and other intellectual works that help to improve the overall community."[17]

Second, the title given to this section also pays homage to a compatriot of mine, Joseph Laycock, and his work *Vampires Today: The Truth About Modern Vampires*, which is quickly becoming a canonical work in the field. Laycock contends, and accurately so I think, that the vampi(y)re, as a category of person, has been defined primarily from the outside, in literature, film, and various popular interest groups. It is only now, after some thirty years of progress, that we've begun to see the vampi(y)re community "take ownership of the category, redefining it from the inside."[18] Under this new definition, the vampi(y)re has transcended myth and the popular imagination, becoming, as Laycock aptly claims, a valid, tangible category of person.

For our purposes here, it is interesting to note that the House of Night's vampyre society shares many similarities with the real vampi(y)re community. For example, fledgling vampyres in general, and Zoey in particular, begin to experience the "Change," including a longing for blood, during their teens. This may also be said about the members of the vampi(y)re community whom I've studied or read about, for they, too, attest to feeling, just after puberty, the

---

[17] For more information, see the representative website of the VVC at: http://www.veritasvosliberabit.com/vvc.html.

[18] Joseph Laycock, *Vampires Today: The Truth About Modern Vampires* (2009).

urge to consume either blood or psychic energy. Another example may be derived from the ceremonial speech given by Neferet during Zoey's first Full Moon Ritual in *Marked*, in which Neferet says to the fledgling vampyres assembled around her that "[t]his is a time when the *veil* between the *mundane* world and the strange and beautiful realms of the Goddess become thin indeed" [italics mine]. Both "veil" and "mundane" are two words that appear frequently in real vampi(y)re discourses. There, the word "veil" generally alludes to "The Black Veil," which is a sort of vampi(y)re code of ethics that has taken prominence in the community. The word "mundane," on the other hand, is in the vampi(y)re community a somewhat elitist term.[19] It refers to most "non-vamps," or as psychic vampire and author Michelle Belanger defines, "people who are entirely focused on [a] material existence to the exclusion of all things spiritual."[20]

In addition, Neferet's ceremonial speech foregrounds two central themes in both the series and the real vampi(y)re community: ritual and magick. To discuss the role they play among vampi(y)res, I must again turn to my astute colleague Joseph Laycock and his groundbreaking work in the field. Laycock contends that, while "[vampi(y)rism] as a whole is not a religion," there do exist "several formal groups within the [vampi(y)re] community that have a primary interest in religion, metaphysics, and magic[k] that would qualify them as [New Religious Movements]."[21]But on the whole, spirituality is, for the members of the vampi(y)re community I've documented, an almost exclusively personal venture. It is independent of the community, yet at the same time it is closely linked to the vampi(y)ric experience of the community's individual members.

I should also add here that Question 155 of the *Vampire & Energy Work Research Survey* (VEWRS), a survey conducted by the Atlanta Vampire Alliance (AVA) to address questions and concerns about the vampi(y)ric experience and community, included a list of fifty-one religions, as well as Pagan and esoteric traditions. The survey instructed the participants, members of the vampi(y)re community, to check all with which they identified. It is worth

---

[19] Laycock, *Vampires Today*.

[20] Michelle Belanger, *The Psychic Vampire Codex: A Manual of Magick and Energy Work* (2004).

[21] Laycock, *Vampires Today*. New Religious Movements are defined by religious scholars as religious or spiritual communities or groups of modern origin.

noting that among the categories marked most frequently by participants in the survey were Magick, Wicca, Neo-Paganism, Occultism, Christianity, and Shamanism.[22] Clearly, these results indicate a strong spiritual connection between the real vampi(y)re community and the vampyre society in House of Night, wherein magick and Wicca are also strong components of the vampyric identity.

Moving on from spiritual matters to more physical ones, the harvesting of human blood by the vampyres in the House of Night series is also of particular interest here. This particular ritual between vampyre and donor, which is kept more or less on the sidelines in the House of Night—we do not know, for instance, where the larger vampyre community obtains its blood—proves equally important in the real vampi(y)re community, as well. Here, just as in the House of Night, it operates under similar secretive terms. During the course of my research, I have documented psychic, blood-drinking, and hybrid vampi(y)res, all of whom use their own methods to harvest and consume (or absorb) blood and/or energy. However, in some cases, blood is stored in a similar stylized fashion as what we observe during the Dark Daughters' ritual led by Aphrodite in *Marked*.

In the case of blood-drinking vampi(y)res in particular, I have documented direct contact feeding (as we've seen in the House of Night series between Zoey and Heath, among others) and the harvesting of human blood into receptacles (similar to the wine goblet used during the ritual in *Marked*), as well as the use of refrigerated blood for consumption in small quantities. In the case of the latter, I may even claim firsthand experience. Some time ago, one of the participants in my study had, on one instance, offered me a sip of his tea "concoction," which he on occasion prepared for himself and drank at such times when fresh human blood was not in ready supply. It was not, of course, until after I had sampled the tea that I learned of its *other* ingredient, much like Zoey and the wine she consumed during her first Dark Daughters ritual (although, unlike Zoey, my response was more one of intrigue than physical ecstasy).

There is one other similarity of note between the vampi(y)re community and the vampyres of the Casts' creation: the name selection and identity-making we observe in the House of Night series. This, I feel, is one of the

---

[22] Suscitatio Enterprises, LLC, "Vampirism and Energy Research Study," http://www.suscitatio.com.

more engaging facets of the series. After all, how many of us have dreamed of leaving behind the boring, day-to-day life we know for another, more fantastical one: a life in which we may pick for ourselves a new name and identity, and embrace our individual differences as a means of unity? As impossible as this fantasy may seem, one has only to look to the real vampi(y)re community and its members for inspiration, some of whom, in the New Orleans and Atlanta communities, I have come to know and communicate with on a personal basis, and therefore offer here as examples: Belfazaar Ashantison, Mephistopheles, Jezabel DeLuna, Maven, and Merticus.

What I hope the reader has gained here is a better understanding not just of the distinct histories of the folkloric revenant, the vampire of popular media, and the real vampi(y)re community, but their importance in fully appreciating the House of Night series' unique and exceptional breed of vampyre. In drawing from older, mythic elements of European revenant folklore along with more recent images of vampires, the Casts have succeeded in creating a modern vampyre—and a modern vampyre society—that has enthralled readers with a thoroughness that even Dracula would envy.

JOHN EDGAR BROWNING is a PhD Candidate in English Writing and Culture and teaches English composition and monster theory at Louisiana State University. He is the coauthor and coeditor of six published and forthcoming books, including: with Caroline Joan (Kay) Picart, *Draculas, Vampires, and Other Undead Forms: Essays on Gender, Race, and Culture* (Scarecrow, 2009); with Picart, *Dracula in Visual Media: Film, Television, Comic Book and Electronic Game Appearances, 1921–2010* (McFarland, 2010); again with Picart, *Speaking of Monsters: A Teratological Anthology* (Palgrave Macmillan, contracted and forthcoming); *Movie Monsters in Print: An Illustrated History* (Schiffer Books, expected 2011); with Judith Kerman, *The Fantastic in Holocaust Literature* (McFarland, contracted and forthcoming); and *The Vampire: His Kith and Kin, A Critical Edition* (Apocryphile Press, expected 2011). Recent works also include several published and forthcoming book chapters and reviews, journal articles, and encyclopedic entries on Dracula, vampires, and horror in such venues as *Film & History*; *Studies in the Fantastic*; *Horror Studies*; *Dead Reckonings: A Review Magazine for the Horror Field*; *Asian Gothic: Essays on Literature, Film, and Anime* (McFarland, 2008); *The Encyclopedia of the Vampire* (Greenwood, 2010); *Schooling Ghouls: Interdisciplinary Approaches to the Pedagogy of Horror* (accepted and forthcoming); and *Open Graves, Open Minds: Vampires and the Undead in Modern Culture* (Manchester University Press, accepted and forthcoming). He has also served as a manuscript referee for *The Journal of Homosexuality* (Routledge-Taylor & Francis) and currently sits on the board of directors for the Empowering Spirits Foundation (ESF), a nonprofit civil rights organization working to achieve lesbian, gay, bisexual, and transgender (LGBT) equality through community service activities. Additionally, Browning has spent the last year conducting an ethnographic study of persons living in New Orleans who self-identify as vampire, a project that has become the focal point of his doctoral dissertation. He is indebted to Leah Wilson, a highly qualified and dedicated editor, for her incredibly helpful suggestions on earlier versions of this chapter.

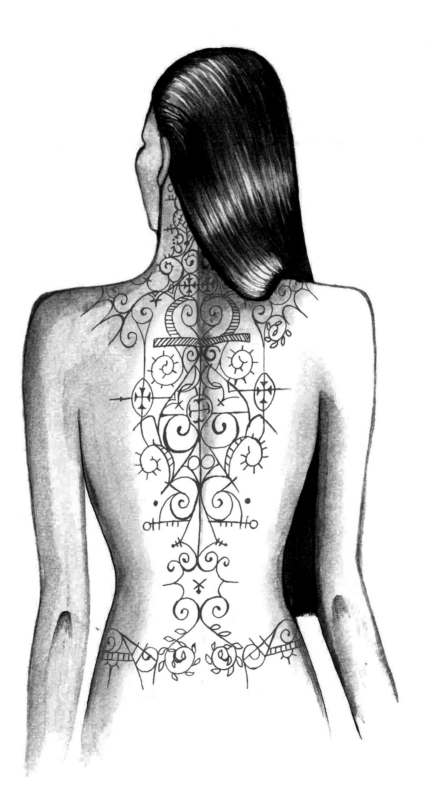

# { By Their Marks You Shall Know Them }

Jana Oliver

WHAT EXACTLY possessed primitive humans to inflict marks on their skin is hard to fathom. Perhaps one of the tribesmen had inadvertently gotten some dirt or ashes in a wound and once it healed, it remained discolored. While sitting around the fire swapping tales, his buddies might have made note of this new thing. With a little experimentation, they realized that if they opened a fresh wound, charred a stick, and buried the black residue inside the slice, the result was a tattoo. Proof that humans are endlessly inventive when they're bored.

Thousands of years later we have a story about a high school girl who is having a rough day: while Zoey Montgomery is trying to cough her lungs out, her best friend is prattling on about Z's drunken "almost" boyfriend and a football game. That all becomes irrelevant when Zoey spies the undead guy standing next to her locker. Don't know about you, but I didn't have dead guys waiting for me in high school. (Not many of the live ones, either.) There's no way Zoey can ignore the newcomer's vivid Mark, the sapphire blue crescent moon tattoo on his forehead, and "the entwining knotwork that framed his equally blue eyes" (*Marked*).

This dude is a Vampyre Tracker, and he's not there to compare notes on Zoey's upcoming geometry test. Instead, he comes equipped with some seriously solemn words for the occasion: "Night has chosen thee; thy death will be thy birth. Night calls to thee; hearken to Her sweet voice. Your destiny awaits you at the House of Night." After a point of his finger and a totally blinding headache, Zoey no longer needs to fret about her exam. She's got bigger worries, as that crescent Mark on her forehead announces to the world she is a fledgling vampyre and belongs in a House of Night.

All because of a tattoo.

## A SHORT HISTORY OF BODY ART

Different types of body art (tattoos, scarification, piercing, henna, and makeup) play different roles depending on the culture, tribe, and individual. From the simple application of makeup to the painful and permanent scarring created by scarification, the results alter not only the skin but society's perception of the skin's owner. Where we in the Western world think nothing of females donning makeup, the act of inserting objects into the skin or having facial tattoos is an entirely different matter. To other cultures, such physical adornments are as common as layering on some foundation and a bit of mascara. Like beauty, tattoos are in the eye of the beholder.

Made by pricking or grooving the skin and adding colored pigment, tattooing has always involved some element of risk even with modern techniques and equipment. The word itself comes from the Tahitian word *tatau*, which means "to mark." The earliest evidence of skin art was found on the Iceman, mummified remains discovered along the Italian-Austrian border in 1991. Ötzi, as he is called, carbon dated at about 5,200 years old.

During their mid-eighteenth century voyages to Tahiti, Captain James Cook's sailors embraced this colorful embellishment, bringing skin art home to European and American societies, where it at first remained primarily confined to the lower classes. Tattoos were considered newsworthy, so explorers would bring home indigenous tribesmen, be they Native Americans, Africans, or Polynesians, to be put on display so that citizens could gawk at the "savages'" tattoos.

It wasn't until the late nineteenth century that European nobility realized they were missing out and began to acquire tattoos themselves. Such notables as King Frederik of Denmark and Czar Nicholas possessed epidermal art. King Edward VII sported a Jerusalem cross in honor of his journey to the Holy Land, and both of his sons (the Duke of Clarence and the future King George V) were tattooed by a Japanese artist. Once royalty took the plunge, it was perfectly acceptable for the upper class to consider adding a mark or two to their own flesh.

In 1891, Samuel Riley created the first tattoo machine by adding an ink chamber and a needle to Thomas Edison's original design for the electric pen, which was used to create stencils to duplicate drawings and handwritten documents. In 1929, Percy Waters modified the pen further, adding an on/off switch, a spark shield, and a needle that could cut plastic stencils. Today's devices can be adjusted for different depths, pressure, and needle speeds, allowing the artist finer control over the final artwork.

Other than certain technological and hygienic advances (antiseptics, disposable needles and inkpots, use of an autoclave to sterilize equipment), the actual tattooing process hasn't really changed that much. Puncturing the dermis with a needle, the artist leaves behind a small dot of insoluble ink. That process, repeated over and over, forms the tattoo. People describe the pain in varying ways, from a pinprick to an intense sunburn. As the skin over the tattoo heals it goes through a molting process, which requires some care to keep the mark from becoming infected. Once healed, depending on its location and its exposure to sunlight and wear, it should remain intact for the remainder of the owner's life.

Though body art was once confined to certain subcultures (gangs, bikers, sailors, circus performers, and other social rebels), it has branched out into the entertainment industry (Angelina Jolie, Cher, and David Beckham, to name a few actors who proudly sport ink). Now going mainstream, one of the fastest-rowing segments of the tattoo industry is suburban, middle-class women. And according to a Pew Research Center survey, over a third of eighteen- to twenty-five-year-olds have at least one tattoo. Between the ages of twenty-six and forty? Forty percent.

Though much about tattoos has changed over the years, some aspects have remained constant. Over the ages skin art has been employed as a form of protection, to ensure health, to commemorate a special event, as an indication of rank or status, as a social statement, or as a declaration of religious faith.

Which brings us to the tattoos in the House of Night series.

## Skin as Canvas

What compels a tattoo artist to choose skin as her medium? Jenny Bunny Bunns, who blogs about her life as a tattoo artist on her website TheInkBunnyDiaries.com, says, "On the creative side, this medium fascinated me because it's art on living skin. Instead of a two-dimensional paper or canvas, I'm working with something that breathes, talks, sweats, stinks (or smells good), moves, etc. It's a challenge in and of itself!" She adds, "My art becomes a part of a living, thinking, feeling being with a life of his/her own. Perhaps on a spiritual level, there is some kind of bond between client and artist." Nyx would approve!

## VAMPS HAVE IT THEIR OWN WAY

Unlike Zoey and her fellow fledglings, we make a conscious decision to be tattooed, even if that decision is made under the influence of fermented beverages. We choose the tattoo's content and placement, as well as when and how we receive it. But in other ways the vampyre tattoos of the House of Night series are very much like ours and serve many of the same functions as they have in the human community, but with a few twists all their own.

In the House of Night series, the tattoo-like Marks are a natural part of becoming a vampyre and appear to be biological in nature. According to Dick Cast (P.C.'s father, who taught high school biology and helped develop the scientific reasoning behind the vampyres' Change), rampant hormonal changes trigger a recessive gene in certain teenagers' bodies. That gene sets in motion a cascade effect of physical symptoms, including increased T-cell production, which in turn destroys the host's capillaries, causing lethal respiratory complications. The series does not explain why the Mark appears in reaction to this biological change, so we are left to speculate on that matter. Is it purely biological? Or is it also mystical, a gift from Nyx?

Vampyre tattoos, unlike ours, aren't static. When a vampyre completes the Change, additional designs are added to the original crescent moon of the Mark. Marks occasionally disappear, reappear, or are altered during the course of the series, but always for compelling reasons. When Stevie Ray rejects the Change in *Betrayed* and dies, she returns to life as something entirely different. When she regains her humanity in *Chosen* and Changes into an adult vampyre, her tattoo becomes something different, as well. Her Mark is described as a "beautiful pattern of tattoos made of swirling flowers with long, graceful stems all twined together . . ." which might signify her affinity for Earth. While that is what one would expect for an adult vampyre, the other change is not: those Marks are the "brilliant scarlet of new blood." The rest of the undead fledglings' Marks, they discover, have changed color, as well.

After her soul is shattered in *Tempted*, Zoey is caught halfway between life and death. To signify that disconnection, her vivid tattoos vanish and she is left with the same crescent moon outline you would expect to find on any other fledgling. Only when she acknowledges every element of her innermost self—A-ya the Cherokee maiden, Brighid, and young Zoey—does she become whole again; her soul reunites with her body, and her special Marks return. That's a powerful statement about Z's journey, and it suggests that while the initial crescent moon Mark itself might be biological, its embellishments are tied to a vampyre's spirit, not his or her body.

Despite those particular differences, the Marks in the House of Night share similarities to their real-world counterparts. Let's explore a few of those commonalities next.

## RITES OF PASSAGE

The Mark first appears at a particular time in life: puberty. Puberty has always been an important milestone in a young male or female's life and is often celebrated by the society in which he or she was raised. The demarcation between a girl and a woman, the onset of menarche, is clearly defined, but not so with a young male. Exactly when a boy becomes a man is difficult to pinpoint, so specific rituals were developed to denote the transition from child to adult.

Tattooing can serve as a test of an individual's fortitude, or identify who has achieved adulthood in the eyes of his/her peers. Some cultures believed that if a boy could not tolerate the pain of tattooing he would not be a fearsome warrior. In other cultures, the marks would not be added to a boy's skin until he had passed some specific test of manhood—in the case of the Ngaju Dayak in Borneo, single-handedly killing a monkey or boar in the jungle using only primitive weapons.

As time passed a young man might continue to have tattoos added to recount important battles, until, when he was quite old, he might have no flesh canvas left to mark. According to an account written in the mid–eighteenth century, one Iroquois chief had sixty tattoos, one for each enemy he'd killed in battle. His skin acted as a walking résumé for anyone able to decipher the symbols. (Zoey's ever-expanding Mark works in a similar way—additional designs form whenever she performs a particularly awesome deed, and her unprecedented lacelike, curling design with "mysterious letter-like symbols" that trails down her shoulders and back adds to her reputation and mystique.)

## Marking the Moment

Skin art is also used to commemorate special events, such as falling in love or having a baby. The inscription of a lover's or child's name or image on a bicep or chest is a powerful statement that that person has changed the wearer's life and will not be forgotten as long as the bearer is alive. It has been estimated that over three-quarters of the soldiers in the early twentieth century tattooed the names of their fallen comrades on their bodies. Often the mark may be nothing more than a date that holds special significance, such as the memorial tattoos that were prevalent after 9/11.

From the moment fledging vampyres are Marked they follow a classic path: they are removed from their ordinary life, go through a period of training, and finally take their place in adult society. The crescent tattoo serves as an initiation into a new world, one rife with emotional turmoil, betrayal, and intrigue. In other words, high school on steroids. Zoey must leave behind her old existence and the majority of her friendships in the human world. She even takes a new name—Zoey Redbird. This is the first rebirth, and the Mark serves as evidence of that moment.

Should the fledgling survive their second, extremely painful rebirth (if Erik's Change in *Chosen* is any indicator) and become an adult vampyre, the crescent moon is filled in and additional tattoos form, trailing down the face. That completed Mark is a badge of honor, signifying that the wearer has endured the rite of passage and lived to tell about it.

## RANK AND STATUS

The completed Mark also serves as notice to the world that this is an adult vampyre, one who has been bound to the Goddess Nyx—in a way, it announces the vampyre's rank, no longer a fledgling but a full-fledged member of society.

Tribes have often used tattoos as an indicator of rank within their community, establishing the pecking order, if you will. The chief might be designated by a series of elaborate marks that signified his place as their leader and perhaps recounted some of the battles that had earned him that position. The upper caste Maori of New Zealand were recognizable through an intricate tattooing procedure called *moko*. Using a small chisel, the tattoo artist carved a series of parallel grooves into the face and body and introduced pigment into them. Highly regarded Maori tattoo artists were paid handsomely in goods— something lower-class individuals couldn't afford.

Women also employed tattoos, often to indicate mating status. When Tahitian girls reached the age of sexual maturity, a black solid mark would be tattooed across their entire buttocks. Until they received the tattoo they were not allowed to engage in sex. To let a young Tahitian male know she was interested, the girl would raise her skirts and display the tattoos. (Christian missionaries, not surprisingly, were shocked by this display of blatant femininity.)

When Zoey enters the House of Night with her Mark filled in, it is an indication of Nyx's favor that everyone recognizes the instant they meet her. Her status as Nyx's Chosen manifests in other ways, such as through her affinity for the elements, but her tattoo makes sure everyone knows who is watching her back.

The color of the red fledglings' Marks also communicates a kind of status. Though the crescent moon on their foreheads indicates their membership in the vampyre community, the color marks them as "other." Blue vamps versus red vamps. The established order versus the outcasts. Or from a human perspective: the scary outcasts versus the *really* scary outcasts.

In our own past, Ancient Rome marked their slaves and criminals so that they might be easily identified and to alert others to the slave's place in the pecking order. If a slave tried to escape, or was caught stealing or lying, certain brands were seared into the forehead so that all might know of the transgression. Though it's tempting to consider that an archaic application, during World War II the Nazis used forearm tattoos to identify their "subhuman" slaves in concentration camps.

## Seeing Red

The color of the red fledglings' Marks deserves special consideration. The authors could easily have allowed Stevie Rae and the others to retain their original sapphire blue Marks and indicate their new Vampyre 2.0 status in other ways. Instead, they chose to change the color of the tattoo. Sapphire blue is calming, a color associated more with melancholy than a feral urge to kill. Red is a powerful color, traditionally used to symbolize blood, violence, and wrath (one of the Seven Deadly Sins), and the change in the red fledglings' Marks sends a clear message that these vampyres are a potential danger to everyone, even their own kind.

## SOCIAL STATEMENTS

The moment you place a mark on your body you acknowledge yourself as a member of one tribe and an outsider to others—you are making a social statement about who you are and where you belong.

Members of street and prison gangs use certain colors of clothing or styles of graffiti when marking their territory to set themselves apart. Gang tattoos transmit similar visual signals to their members and to those who would oppose them. But it's not just their rivals they're sending a message to. According to GangInk.com, an online resource for gang tattoos, "gang members in particular take pride in branding themselves as outside of the boundaries of conventional society."

### Going Bold

Now that tattooing has gone mainstream, those seeking to make a bolder social statement often turn to scarification. This process (branding, cutting, or slicing patterns into the upper levels of the skin to cause extensive scarring) is not for the faint of heart. In the Sepik region of Papua New Guinea, for example, young males are sliced on their backs, chest, and buttocks with a sharpened piece of bamboo, an excruciatingly lengthy and painful process. The resulting pattern represents the teeth marks of a crocodile, who the tribesmen believed created humans—their way of paying homage to the divine.

Most often seen in the sub-Saharan African cultures because the high melanin content of the skin makes tattooing difficult, scarification has crossed over the oceans to Europe and America. Gays and lesbians in San Francisco in the 1980s were early adopters, and the art form spread across the country in the 1990s.

No matter the reason you choose to have skin art (or in the case of vampyres, whether you choose it at all), a tattoo sets you apart—and that can have very real social consequences. Employers (Starbucks, for instance) may hire someone with ink, but require that it be covered so as not to offend their customers. What is a statement of belonging in one context can be evidence of difference—and an excuse for discrimination—in another.

Belonging to the vampyre community makes you special; fledglings join a culture with a rich history they can be proud of. Still, a Mark comes with immediate social consequences. After Zoey's encounter with the Tracker, her best friend, Kayla, reacts to her first Mark with horror and disgust, as if Zoey has suddenly become a different person. In the eyes of the humans, that analogy isn't far wrong. In a sense the old Zoey is no more; she's now a creature of the night. And superstitions, like vampyres, are hard to kill.

Zoey's new Mark brands her as a symbol of evil in her parents' eyes. Her stepfather sees it and immediately proclaims her Satan. That isn't literary license on the part of the authors: some fundamentalist churches believe that tattoos in any form are the mark of hell, that tattoo studios are demonic, and that only the ungodly would wear such things on their skin (though these hard-line views have been countered by other Christians who feel that tattoos are no more inherently evil than other forms of body decoration).

## RELIGION AND SPIRITUALITY

Tattooing for a spiritual purpose is as old as religion itself. For early humans, tattoos involved fire, blood, and physical discomfort, all of which invoke strong spiritual and sacrificial themes, potent elements in which to catch the attention of the gods. If the deities were pleased, you would thrive. If not, maybe you needed another tattoo.

Tattoos could also help you after death, as well. In Sioux culture, it was believed that upon a warrior's demise he would mount a ghost horse and ride toward the land of "Many Lodges." During that journey he would encounter an old woman who would bar his way. If he could not show her certain tattoos, the warrior would be returned to this world to wander as a ghost for eternity.

## A Tattoo a Day

Tattoos weren't just good for your spiritual health. Some researchers believe the tattoos might have had a therapeutic purpose—that they may have been a primitive version of over-the-counter medications. The mummy of Ötzi the Iceman mentioned earlier had over fifty separate tattoos. Of particular significance is where they were located: along the lumbar spine and knee and ankle joints. This placement perhaps indicates an effort to combat arthritis or other joint ailments. Ojibwa Indians here in North America who suffered from headaches or toothaches would inscribe permanent marks on the cheeks, temples, and forehead to try to counteract their pain.

Some cultures believed that you could invoke the protection of a particular animal by marking its image into the flesh, an important survival tactic in a world where humans were considered tasty two-legged meals. Tattooing the image of an animal on your skin acted as a talisman of sorts, or might even permit you to take on that animal's attributes, melding them with your own. A fox tattoo, for instance, would instill that beast's supposed cunning in the recipient, an owl its wisdom or a lion its strength. According to Cherokee tradition, painting or tattooing an eagle's eyes around your own would gift you with that raptor's keen eyesight.

Even Christianity used to look favorably on tattoos. After completing the arduous journey to the Holy Land, early believers would acquire a tattoo on their hands or face to commemorate their pilgrimage and to actively display their piety to the world. The practice fell out of favor during Emperor Constantine's reign (A.D. 306-337). No doubt drawing on the injunction against marks as mentioned in Leviticus 19:28, the emperor felt such tattoos disfigured "that made in God's image." By A.D. 787, tattoos had been banned in England, and during the Dark and Middle Ages those with marks were viewed as outsiders, and, in some cases, evil incarnate.

Some of today's Christians display their faith through marks, and it is not uncommon to find figures of Jesus, Mary, the fish symbol, crosses, angels, and Bible verses tattooed on the observant. Jews display their faith by inscribing verses in Hebrew, the Magen David (Star of David), or scenes from the Old Testament on their flesh (though traditionally, having a tattoo means you cannot be buried in a Jewish cemetery). Despite Islam's prohibition against marks, some Muslims have tattooed passages from the Koran, the Crescent Star, and the Hand of Fatima, which is supposed to ward off the evil eye. For Pagans, you'll find a vast array of ink art: deities, Celtic knots, Odin's triple horns, lunar crescents, and an astonishing selection of animals, both real and mythical.

The House of Night's tattoos obviously have a spiritual tie; however, the vampyres' Marks don't just reflect their devotion to Nyx but are directly connected to the Goddess herself. Nyx serves as a divine tattoo artist, shaping the raw clay of the fledgling, marking the body both physically and spiritually, and preparing him or her for a life in Nyx's service.

It is possible that Nyx has no say in who becomes a vampyre, or perhaps with the aid of biology Nyx selects certain humans and sets them on a path to become her children. Either way, the tattoos seal the relationship between goddess and acolyte. Zoey's more elaborate tattoos are evidence of her special relationship with the goddess; her tattoos are more than just a "this girl has potential" stamp of approval. From a metaphysical perspective, Zoey's Marks are a physical road map of her journey along Nyx's path as she grows into her role as High Priestess.

## STATEMENTS OF INDIVIDUAL IDENTITY

Within the House of Night books, adult vampyres' Goddess-given Marks range from the mysterious to the elegant. High Priestess Neferet's tattoos are described as cresting ocean waves, while those of Zoey's fencing teacher (Professor Langford) favor the more dramatic approach: "His tattoo represented two dragons whose bodies, serpent-like, wrapped down over his jaw line. Their heads were over his brows and their mouths open, breathing fire at the crescent moon" (sounds amazing) (*Marked*). Other professors have thin Celtic knots and feathers or plunging horses. Not surprisingly, the latter belongs to the equestrian teacher, Professor Lenobia. Erik's full tattoo is "a stunning pattern of interlocking knots that formed the shape of a mask," signaling his love of acting (*Chosen*). In the world of the House of Night, Marks are unique to the individuals who wear them, clear reflections of their owners' identities: their passions, personalities, and destinies.

This is often the case for tattoos in the real world, especially today. Tattoos are a chance for people to express their individuality and their interests: a favorite hobby, sports team, entertainer, or animal (cats anyone?). Pop culture, too, supplies ample inspiration for skin art. The Casts have encountered ardent fans of the House of Night who have acquired crescent tattoos in homage to the series. Numerous fans of Sherrilyn Kenyon's Dark-Hunter® books have adopted Artemis' double bow and arrow symbol (as worn by the Dark-Hunters in the series) as part of their permanent epidermal wardrobe.

## A NOTE ON PLACEMENT

We've talked a lot about the purpose of tattoos, but the placement often has special significance, as well. Fertility marks located on a woman's lower abdomen or on her thighs might enhance her sexuality, while tattoos on a male's chest and back signify prowess. Marks along the temple or the jaw might indicate a need for healing or, especially if highly visible, might serve as a warning of the wearer's magical or physical abilities.

Tattoos, by their nature, can be put just about anywhere there is skin, though some parts of the body are more sensitive than others, making the process more painful. So why would countless cultures choose to mark their faces when there are plenty of other areas available? What drives the Maori in New Zealand, the aboriginal Kondhs of India, and the Inuit in the Arctic to put those tattoos in plain sight?

In part, it's a human thing—we check out each other's faces the moment we meet and make certain subjective assessments based on what we see. We determine, in a fraction of a second, if the newcomer is a potential friend or foe, a member of our own race or community, and what their expression might hold in store for us. We decide if that person is trustworthy based on what we "read" on his or her face. Tattoos help this process along. (For some North American Indian tribes, tattoos helped members differentiate between fellow warrior and foe during the heat of battle, thereby sparing a warrior the embarrassing realization that he had just speared one of his own guys.) When the tattoo is on the face, the identification process will be even quicker.

In the House of Night series, the crescent moon is front and center in the middle of the forehead, and is impossible to ignore unless obscured by makeup. But the Mark is also located at the Anja, the sixth chakra. This chakra (also referred to as the third eye) is symbolized by the colors violet, deep blue, or indigo, which are remarkably close to the sapphire blue of most vampyre tattoos. The Anja is considered the center of intuition, responsible for the evaluation of past experiences, clairvoyance, and the ability to separate fantasy from reality. The chakra's aspect is self-realization, which is one of the fledglings' primary goals at the House of Night (aside from survival). The profound changes occurring both inside the body and without require the fledgling to reassess everything he or she has held as truth and find new ways to interact with the world. I can't imagine a more appropriate place for that tattoo.

## WHY TATTOOS MATTER

In both our world and Zoey's, tattoos tell a tale of courage and of pain endured. Marking our skin shows us to be part of a community, but also that we are a separate and unique person with particular interests and experiences. It gives a visual proclamation as to who we are and where and to whom we belong.

No matter the reason for acquiring a tattoo, when it is placed on our flesh, it changes us. It is a visceral and visual acknowledgement that "this is my body and I choose it to be beautiful, but according to my rules." As we wait to see what Zoey's future holds in store, we can rest assured that as she discovers more about herself and her destiny, her Marks will continue to be a compelling and meaningful part of that journey.

JANA OLIVER has the perfect job—she listens to the voices in her head and then writes their stories. Her latest creation is the young adult Demon Trappers series (St. Martin's Press) set in a dystopian 2018 Atlanta and populated by Hellspawn, Deaders, and scheming necromancers.

Jana's foray into time travel and alternate history resulted in the multi-award winning Time Rovers series (Dragon Moon Press). Based in 1888 London, the series deftly blends time travel, shape-shifters, and Jack the Ripper. Visitors are always welcome at her website: www.JanaOliver.com.

# { The Divine Cat }

## Ellen Steiber

I MIGHT as well admit my prejudice up front: I've been crazy about cats for as long as I can remember, and I've been lucky enough to live with them for most of my life. So one of the things that immediately drew me into the House of Night series was the cats. Cats everywhere, roaming freely, and always welcome in the dorms, cafeteria, stables, and even the classrooms—basically my idea of the perfect school. Then I was completely charmed by Nala, the sneezey, often grumpy, little cat who chooses Zoey for her own. P.C. and Kristin Cast clearly know and love their cats, and it's a delight to see how they use them in these books. Not only do they create very real felines—sweet, moody, comforting, and impossible to predict or control—but they make creative use of some of the mythic and mystical lore that has been part of feline history for the last 5,000 years. Though the House of Night cats are not, on their own, magical in the traditional sense, they draw on a rich history of cat mythology and folklore.

Leonardo da Vinci once wrote, "The smallest feline is a masterpiece." Cats are incredibly well-designed, beautiful little predators who can live with or without us. With their lithe, muscular bodies, they're capable of leaping, running, climbing to great heights, and moving almost silently. Compared to humans, they have heightened senses of smell, hearing, vision, and balance. They can sense seismic vibrations long before we do, and they sense magnetic and meteorological changes far more keenly. They clearly know things that we don't. When provoked or when courting, they are capable of making the most dreadful sounds; listening to one or more cats caterwauling can raise the hair on the back of your neck.

Although domestic cats are fairly small animals who live with us quite peaceably, they're not all that far removed from their larger cousins, the wild cats. Much like vampyres, cats retain a fierce, savage nature beneath a civilized surface. As the writer Carl Van Vechten put it in the title of his book, the cat is *The Tiger in the House*. All felines, from house cats to lions, share the same basic body structure, the same supple movements, the same hunting instincts, and a wild, independent nature that never completely disappears no matter how long or closely they live with us.

They're resilient creatures with a knack for survival that includes an uncanny ability to land on their feet, even when falling from great heights, due to the cat's agile spine and tail (the tail can whip around and turn the body so that the cat lands feetfirst). Cats have also been known to travel great distances to return to their homes, and to survive many natural disasters, contributing to the belief that cats have nine lives.

Naturally nocturnal, they're wired to hunt at night. Although cats can't see in complete darkness, their pupils change size and shape, allowing them to see with very little light. A layer of cells in the cat's retina, the tapetum, collects and reflects light back into the eye, acting like a mirror and causing a strange effect called "eyeshine" in which the cat's eyes seem to glow. These extraordinary feline eyes have fascinated and frightened humans for centuries, and we've attached many beliefs to this phenomenon: that cats are connected to the moon, which also waxes and wanes in size; that cats—lions in particular—are able to look at the setting sun and keep its light in their eyes; that cats can see the future or see into the spirit world; and that cats can see into our minds and thoughts.

That's a lot of mystical power for one small creature. Perhaps because of that perceived power, stories about cats throughout history have had a dual nature. We've seen them as creatures of light and dark, friends and enemies, demons and saviors. Few people are neutral about cats even today. Humans seem to love them or hate them, and the hatred is almost always intertwined with fear. People fear dogs as well, but that fear is usually simple and physical: they're afraid of being bitten. The fear of cats, though, seems to go beyond being bitten or scratched to an underlying belief that cats are aloof, devious, and somehow evil creatures who intend to do us harm.

The House of Night vampyres, of course, don't fear cats. They see them as beloved companions and allies, a connection to their Goddess. In fact, the House of Night cats function a great deal like witches' familiars. In order to understand cats as familiars—and to understand their ancient connection with magic and the supernatural—it helps to go back to an earlier historical belief about cats: that they were not just animals but gods.

## THE CAT GODDESSES

"Thousands of years ago, cats were worshipped as gods. Cats have never forgotten this."

—Anonymous

Western cat lore seems to officially begin in Ancient Egypt, where for over two thousand years cats were worshipped. The Egyptians had several feline divinities. The most beloved was Bast (also known as Bastet and Pasht), a benevolent goddess who was considered a protector and a healer. Sekhmet was the bloodthirsty, lion-headed goddess of war and destruction. Tefnut, yet another lion-headed divinity, was a goddess of rain and mists who, like Sekhmet, was capable of turning herself into a devouring lion. Mafdet, who was worshipped in very early times, was not only a feline goddess of judicial authority, but a protector against snakes.

The Egyptians valued cats for reasons that were both practical and mystical. On a practical level, cats kept mice, rats, and even snakes out of homes and the storehouses where grain was kept. Cats were also considered magical creatures, primarily for their ability to see in the dark. The Egyptians feared darkness and believed that since cats' eyes wax and wane like the moon, cats themselves were a kind of protection against the dark of night. Bast was considered a moon goddess, an enemy of darkness, who held the sun's light in her eyes at night. Like the moon, cats were believed to have the power to control tides, weather, and the growth of crops. The Egyptians also believed that a cat's eyes could see into the human mind and soul, and sometimes even predict whether or not someone who was sick would recover. The Egyptian word for cat, *mau*, meant "to see."

How exactly did cats become gods? Scholars think the animals were first brought into Egypt by the Ethiopians. We know cats were being worshipped at least 5,000 years ago, because the earliest portrait of Bast was found in a temple built in the Fifth Dynasty, around 3000 B.C. Bast is usually portrayed either as a cat or with a woman's body and a cat's head. (There are also statues of her with a lion's head, which are easily confused with statues of Sekhmet.) Bast usually wore a long dress and carried an aegis or shield, as well as a sistrum, which was a kind of rattle used in the worship of Isis.

## A Cat Goddess in Florida?

A sixteenth-century wooden sculpture known as the Key Marco Cat was excavated on Florida's Marco Island in 1895 by anthropologist Frank Hamilton Cushing. The six-inch-tall carving shows a slender kneeling human body with a cat's head. The figure is leaning slightly forward, hands on knees, as if listening to a particularly interesting conversation. No one really knows who carved the Key Marco Cat or which culture it belonged to, but the best guess is that it's connected with the Calusa, a Native American people who lived in Florida between the eighth and sixteenth centuries, and that the wooden figurine survived because it was buried in a bog. (Or perhaps it survived because cats have nine lives.) We also have no idea whether the Calusa regarded cats as gods or spirit protectors, but the figurine seems to be a kind of aesthetic kin to the statues of the Egyptian cat gods. The Key Marco Cat now resides in the Smithsonian Institution.

Bast was believed to be the daughter of two of the most powerful figures in the Egyptian pantheon: Isis, the goddess of motherhood, fertility, and magic, and her husband, Osirus, the sun god who ruled the Underworld and protected the souls of the dead. By 950 B.C., Bast was a goddess in her own right, with the combined powers of her divine parents. Like Isis, she was a goddess of fertility, sexuality, and magic identified with the moon. Like Osirus, she was a sun god and a protector of the dead. As a sun god, Bast was a symbol of life and light, of the warm rays of the sun that make crops grow. She was also a healer.

All cats were considered direct links to Bast, and thus sacred. A cat in the house was believed to bring the goddess' divine favor and protection against misfortune. Household cats were treated with great respect, often allowed to eat from their masters' plates. It was forbidden, under the penalty of death, to kill a cat even by accident. If a house cat died, the family went into mourning, shaving their eyebrows and beating their breasts at the funeral. Even the poor were expected to give their cats a proper burial. Temple cats, which were considered actual representations of the goddess, received the most elaborate funerals of all. Their bodies were mummified and placed in sarcophagi, usually with a bowl of milk. It was believed that the priests' prayers kept these bowls filled in the afterlife.

The lion-headed goddess Sekhmet, whose name means the "Mighty One," was also a solar god, but she represented fire and the scorching, devouring rays of the sun. Statues of Sekhmet show a female lion or a woman with a lion's head, often crowned by a solar disk. A fiery glow was said to come from her body, and the hot, desert winds were her breath. Sekhmet came into the world with a dark purpose: to destroy the enemies of Ra. Ra, who was sometimes referred to as the "Great Cat," was another sun god and king of all the Egyptian gods. It was said he created Sekhmet from the fire in his eye in order to punish humans who had sinned. A warrior goddess known as the "Crusher of Hearts," Sekhmet spread terror and plagues and was one of the most bloodthirsty deities in any pantheon. When Ra initiated the Slaying of Mankind to punish humans who rebelled against him, Sekhmet killed so eagerly and savagely that even Ra, who had asked for her aid in the slaughter, saw that if she continued, humankind would be wiped out. He had to trick her in order to stop her—he got her drunk.

But that was hardly the end of Sekhmet's influence. Her image appeared on temple doorways as a guardian of wisdom. In the millennia that followed she was worshipped as a deity of fate, associated with magic and sorcery. Because of her powers of sorcery, she was prayed to as a great healer, a goddess of child-birth, and a patron of bonesetters. Still, she never lost her taste for blood. Her favorite sacrifices were children.

Cat worship continued in Egypt until the time of the Romans. It was against the law to take cats out of Egypt, but Phoenician traders managed to smuggle them into Rome, where they became very popular for their ability to kill mice and rats. But as they became more common throughout the ancient world, they were no longer considered quite so divine.

## The Jaguar God

The Egyptians weren't the only culture who held cats sacred. Tepeyollotl, worshipped by Mexico's Aztec and Zapotec peoples as well as in Guatemala, was described as a monster jaguar who would leap out and seize the setting sun. His name meant "Heart of the Mountains" or the "Lord of the Mountains." The jaguar, like Bast, was connected with vegetation and fertility.

Here's the thing about gods and goddesses: they're shape-shifters of a sort. They've been around for millennia, and over time, as populations have moved from place to place (by force or by choice), or as the needs of the culture changed, the gods have moved and changed, too. They're given different names, but the "new" gods or goddesses often take on the powers of the old. One example of this is Bast taking on the powers of Isis and Osiris, as some scholars think Bast is just the feline form of Isis. Sekhmet, too, is believed by some to be just another aspect of Bast, her shadow or dark twin. Scholars believe that in ancient Greece, the cat goddess became known as Artemis, the moon goddess and hunter; and in Rome, she became Diana. Artemis was not a sun god at all—those powers were given to her twin brother, Apollo—but she was a virgin goddess who ruled over the moon, like Bast, and childbirth, like Sekhmet. Though the cat was only one of the animals Artemis was associated with, when the giant Typhon stormed Olympus and the terrified gods fled to Egypt, each of them disguised in animal form, Artemis took the form of a cat.

What we see here is a concept that's at the heart of the House of Night series—the idea that the Goddess has been with us since the dawn of time, taking on different forms in different cultures. She has been known as Isis and Bast and Sekhmet, Nyx and Artemis and Hecate and Selene, Freya and Hel, and eventually Mary, mother of Christ. From the Egyptians on, cats were connected with many of these forms of the goddess. But as Goddess worship fell out of favor, so did cats.

## CAT FAMILIARS

"Ah! cats are a mysterious kind of folk. There is more passing in their minds than we can be aware of. It comes no doubt from their being so familiar with warlocks and witches."

—Sir Walter Scott

During the Middle Ages, the old religions of Ancient Greece and Rome, and of pagan Britain, Scandinavia, and Germany, gave way to Christianity. The church was determined that it be the one and only religion, and so it took over sites sacred to other faiths. Churches were built where shrines, sacred woods, or sacred wells once stood, and many things connected with these earlier religions—especially the worship of the Goddess and nature spirits—were demonized.

We can see this clearly in the evolution of Freya, the Norse goddess of love, beauty, pleasure, fertility, and marriage, a sort of Scandinavian Aphrodite with traces of Bast. Freya was also a warrior goddess. After a battle, she led the god Odin's handmaidens to the battlefields so they could choose the most valorous among those slain and lead them to Odin's hall, Valhalla. It was Freya's right to claim half of those who had died and bring them to her hall, Sessrumnir, a heavenly afterlife where the dead warriors experienced so much pleasure that wives and sisters were said to join them in battle, hoping they'd also wind up in Freya's hall. (Those chosen for Valhalla would have to get ready to fight all over again in Ragnarok, the great, final battle the Norse believed would result in the destruction of the world. Really, wouldn't you rather go with the goddess?)

Freya had several ways of traveling, but her best-known was a chariot drawn by two cats. Some sources say these cats were black and others blue—which means gray when you're talking cat colors. From what I can tell, when she came to take the dead to her hall, Freya always traveled via cat chariot. What fascinates me about this image is that instead of being the goddess herself, cats are now the *vehicle* of the goddess. They literally bring the divine to you, especially at the time of death. It's *through the cats* that we meet the goddess and are taken by her to the heavenly realm. (Apparently, P.C. Cast was also fascinated by Freya's cat connection. According to *The Fledgling Handbook 101*, Freya was one of Nyx's vampyre High Priestesses—I should have known!—and the cats that pulled her chariot were her familiars in the same way Nala is Zoey's.)

## The Cat That Predicts Death

We may have a modern-day equivalent of Freya's cats. Oscar, a cat who resides in a New England nursing home, is almost always found curled against a patient's side in the hours before the patient's death. According to a 2009 article published in *The New England Journal of Medicine*, Oscar seems to have an uncanny ability to "predict" death and to be there to give comfort to the dying. Perhaps like Freya's cats, he is there to bring them to the Goddess.

During the Middle Ages, when the church became the preeminent political and religious power throughout Europe, Freya changed. In medieval German stories she was transformed from a beautiful goddess with long golden hair to a wrinkled old hag who was cruel and bloodthirsty. She became known as a witch. And cats, because they were sacred to Freya, became demons or witches' familiars.

The term "familiar" dates back to the thirteenth century, when it was believed that a spirit—usually a demon—could embody itself in animal form to serve as a protector or companion to a human. The human was usually said to be a witch or a sorcerer who had used magic to summon the evil spirit, and the familiar often took the form of a cat. Familiars were supposedly psychically connected to the witch and helped her work spells. The belief expanded into the idea that witches could change themselves into cats, and any cat might be a witch's familiar or even the witch herself. In medieval times, when people suspected of witchcraft were being tortured and burned at the stake, these beliefs were not a good thing for cats.

Many of those who were branded witches were originally priestesses of the cults that still worshipped the Goddess and nature spirits. Most were devotees of the moon goddess in one of her many forms and were considered "wise women," who knew the healing properties of plants and herbs. When the church recast these priests and priestesses as sorcerers and witches, they also recast nature spirits, fairies, and elves as demons. Black cats, in particular, because of their connection with the witchy Freya, were considered omens of death.

## The Marcaou

In France, some people believed in the demonic Marcaou cats, born to the Fairies, that would poison unlucky humans then wait by the dying humans' beds to carry the spirits to hell. The Fairy queens themselves gave birth to Margotines, beautiful white courtier cats that could shape-shift into attractive young women and bewitch unsuspecting men as they slept.

To be anything other than Christian was evil. In medieval England, around A.D. 906, a cult called the Daughters of Diana was said to celebrate Sabbats four times a year. These were rituals connected with the moon and designed to bring fertility to humans, animals, and plants. To the Daughters of Diana, the moon was represented by her Egyptian symbol, the cat, and so these "witches" would dress themselves as cats. The church claimed that rather than just dressing as cats, they could change themselves into cats. They also claimed that the witches' tabby cats would transform into coal-black steeds on which the witches would gallop along the country roads—when not riding broomsticks, of course. This cult of the goddess—along with its cats—was persecuted and wiped out.

The church was exceptionally clever and thorough in stirring up the terror of witches. They convinced people that these women (and occasionally men) had the powers of the moon and could control the tides and planting cycles, and even drive people to lunacy. Cats were said to share these powers, which made them equally evil and dangerous. In 1232, Pope Gregory IX formally decreed domestic cats diabolical.

The Casts touch on this in *Untamed*, when Aphrodite notes angrily to Sister Mary Angela that the church used to kill off cats for being witches and demons, and the nun replies, "Don't you think that's because cats have always been so closely associated with women? Especially those considered wise women by the general public. So naturally, in a predominantly male-dominated society, a certain type of people would see sinister things in them."

What exactly was the church's problem with women? It all goes back to Eve. It was Eve, the church literally believed, who tempted Adam to disobey God in the Garden of Eden. Women's sexuality was considered a tool of the Devil, designed to lead men away from God and into sin. (The church has never been comfortable with sex unless it was sex for reproduction within the bounds of marriage.) You can see why goddesses—especially beautiful, sexual, pleasure-loving goddesses like Freya—were considered threats by the church. She was the embodiment of so many things that the male-dominated clergy hated and feared.

## A Superstition with Nine Lives?

When I was growing up in the 1960s, a girl told me that our family had to get rid of our cat because it would suck the breath from my infant sister. The superstition is ridiculous, of course: the structure of a cat's jaws makes it anatomically impossible for a cat to suck anything. But it's an old and widely held belief that may go as far back as the stories of Lilith. According to a Jewish legend that became popular during the Middle Ages, Lilith was Adam's first wife, who refused to obey him and so was cast out of the Garden of Eden and became a demon. Lilith, who was said to suck the life from infants as they slept, often appeared as an owl or a cat.

Despite the church's longstanding antipathy for women and cats, things didn't really come to a head for a few centuries. In 1489, Pope Innocent VIII wrote the *Malleus Maleficarum* ("Hammer for Witches"), which declared that children of Satan tended to turn themselves into animals, just as Satan had turned himself into a serpent in order to tempt Eve. The ecclesiastical courts soon began charging women with having turned themselves into cats. In 1596, in Aberdeen, Scotland, a group of women were accused of being witches who had turned themselves into cats, allegedly to celebrate an orgy at a place called Fish Cross, named for a cross that stood in the middle of a fish market. Somehow, it never occurred to the church authorities that the orgy-seeking "witches" might have been actual cats drawn to the area by the smell of fish.

It was between the sixteenth and eighteenth centuries, however, that the Christian world became positively obsessed with the fear of witches. Nearly every unfortunate occurrence was blamed on them—lightning, disease, fire, hail, even shipwrecks. In 1607, Isobel Grierson was burned for witchcraft after a man claimed that she entered his house disguised as his own cat, but accompanied by other cats that were all caterwauling, nearly scaring him and his wife to death. (Was it possible his cat was in heat and followed by toms?) Poor Isobel was then accused of visiting another man's house in cat form and spraying his wife. This woman later died, obviously because she had been sprayed by Isobel. There are, in fact, a remarkable number of accounts of men who saw women change themselves into cats and men who claimed to be wounded by cats. And there are also quite a number of confessions from witches claiming they became cats, but it's nearly certain that most of these were obtained under torture. One woman in England was hanged because a neighbor saw a cat jump up onto her windowsill, and was convinced it was the devil.

Reading the history of cats in Europe can give you nightmares. As victims of the witch hysteria, cats were put on trial and convicted, whipped, burned, boiled, drowned, and walled-in alive. They had gone from being creatures who were worshipped as gods to creatures that, because they were linked with the Goddess, were feared and destroyed.

## That Old Black Magic

During this period, there were people who were actually practicing black magic, and they, too, killed and tormented cats and used feline body parts in their spells, giving some truth to the church's claims. These devotees of the black arts believed that the cat's ability to see spirits was contained in some part of their body—usually the eyes or skin—and that ability could be transferred to a human if the human ate the body part or wore it as a talisman. Sometimes, in an effort to gain this "second sight," the ashes of burnt cats were ground into an ointment and applied to the eyes, or the cats were simply offered as sacrifices to the gods of darkness. Even as recently as 1923, the British occultist Aleister Crowley, a sadist who hated cats, was believed to have transfixed a cat through magic and then sacrificed it in a ritual to cure his hepatitis.

I know. This all sounds gross beyond belief, but it's not that different from what's still going on in Asia. One reason that tigers are currently endangered is that poachers are killing them in order to sell their body parts for potions that are supposed to do everything from strengthening bones to curing arthritis to working as an aphrodisiac.

What finally put an end to the persecution of cats in the West—and it took centuries—was the realization that cats were essential in stopping the waves of bubonic plague that were devastating Europe. It wasn't understood then that rats and mice carried fleas, which spread the plague. Gradually, though, people began to notice that there weren't as many deaths in households with cats, and they finally made the rat-flea-disease connection. After that, cats were considered invaluable in the fight against the plague. Even the church had to acknowledge this and finally put an end to burning them.

Yet even throughout these times when cats were so widely feared, beliefs in cats as beneficent creatures with mystical powers that allowed them to predict the future or bring good luck remained. Throughout the British Isles, a cat sneezing or washing itself behind its ears with a wet forepaw was a sign of rain; a cat sitting with its back to the fire, a sign of coming frost. It was also said that a black cat would bring a maiden her lover, and that a cat sneezing on a wedding day was a good omen for the bride. Traces of beliefs in magical "helper" cats can still be found in the European fairy tales. Check out Charles Perrault's "Puss in Boots" or Madame d'Aulnoy's "Queen Cat" (also known as "White Cat") in which courtly, elegant cats are not only lucky but save the people they love from misfortune. In the South of France, people believed in Matagot, or "magician" cats that would bring prosperity into a house where they were loved and wellcared for (though according to one French fairy tale, "The Black Cat," all cats are magicians). Some stories claim that the Matagot were enemies of the demonic fairy cats, the Marcaou, but more typical are good-luck stories, like the popular tale of "Dick Whittington and His Cat."

## MAGICAL CATS IN OTHER CULTURES

"Who can believe that there is no soul behind those luminous eyes?"
—Theophile Gautier

It wasn't only the medieval Europeans who believed that cats were magical. In Islamic lore, the djinn were supernatural creatures who could take the form of animals, and frequently appeared as—or lived inside of—cats. Having free will, djinn could be good or bad. Sometimes they brought their humans wealth and good fortune; other times, they tormented them. Humans seemed to gain a djinn's help either by making offerings to them or enslaving them. (The "genie" in the story of Aladdin's Lamp is an example of a djinn.) However, treating a djinn badly could result in the djinn taking revenge. The ancient Persians were reluctant to kill cats, fearing there might be a djinn inside. If they killed the cat and freed the djinn, the djinn were likely to spend eternity avenging themselves on the one who'd destroyed their habitat. An old Egyptian legend warns that a djnn takes the form of a cat in order to a haunt a house.

## The First Cat

Islamic lore also gives us a lovely legend that traces the origin of cats to Noah's ark. The story goes that the two mice on the ark were reproducing so quickly that Noah soon had a serious problem. So he went to the female lion on board and passed his hand three times over her head. She then sneezed out a cat—undoubtedly the ancestor of Zoey's sneezy cat Nala—and the mouse problem was soon solved.

Another legend says that the Prophet Mohammed so loved his own cat Muezza that he blessed her, giving all cats the ability to land on their feet when they fall, and giving them all a permanent place in the Islamic Paradise.

In Mesoamerica and South America, jaguars are believed to able to travel easily between our realm and the spirit realm. Because of this, the jaguar is considered a kind of familiar, a spirit companion of great strength known as a *nagual*. During shamanic rituals, when the shaman enters the spirit realm—usually to heal others—he calls on his nagual to protect him from evil spirits and to fight any evil that might threaten him or those he's trying to help. During these spirit journeys, the shaman shape-shifts, taking the form of the jaguar in order to cross over into the spirit realm.

In medieval China and Japan, cats were also accorded mystical powers. Cats are believed to have been smuggled into China from Egypt as early as the third century. It took another 600 years for them to show up in Japan, where they were imported from China and Korea. Cats got mixed reviews in these countries. It seems most of the folklore about them depicts them as demons—stealing from humans, shape-shifting from cat to woman and back again, wielding dancing balls of fire, and frightening people by walking two-legged across their roofs. There were also spectre-cats—the ghosts of cats—that delighted in haunting humans (though in Japan, tortoiseshell cats were believed to keep ghosts away. Go figure!). In China it was believed that after death humans turned into cats. Carl VanVechten tells of the Empress Wu, who decreed that no cats could enter her palace after she executed a court lady who had "threatened to turn the empress into a rat and tease her as a spectre-cat" (a story that can be found in Carl Van Vechten's *The Tiger in the House*).

In Japan, some cats were believed to be goblins and others, protectors against goblins. The famous story "The Boy Who Drew Cats" tells of cats painted on temple screens who came to life to defeat a giant rat goblin. Japanese cats also had a reputation for turning into beautiful women, who sometimes helped their owners—one story tells of a cat who turned into a geisha to earn money for the impoverished old couple who owned her—and sometimes turned out to be demons. Long-tailed cats, in particular, were considered capable of turning into demons, and one Japanese demon, the *nekomata*, was said to be an enormous cat with a forked tail.

## *Long Before Dracula* . . .

"The Vampire Cat of Nabeshima," which dates back the Sengoku Era (1568-1615), tells of the Prince of Hizen, who had a beautiful consort named O Toyo living in his household. One night an enormous cat (with a normal tail) appeared in O Toyo's bedroom, sprang at her, and crushed her throat in its teeth until she died. The cat dug a grave beneath one of the verandas and buried O Toyo's body. It then shape-shifted, taking on O Toyo's form. The prince never realized that his lover was dead. Night after night, the false O Toyo came into his bedchamber and drained the blood from him. The prince soon became sickly and weak and suffered from terrifying nightmares. He had no idea that he was sleeping with a vampire instead of his beloved consort. The prince's retainers guessed that something was attacking him at night, but whenever they kept watch over him, they fell asleep—bewitched by the vampire cat. Eventually, with the help of a priest, one of the prince's young retainers managed to stay awake and fight the false O Toyo, who turned back into a cat and vanished into the mountains.

(A more complete version of this story can be found in *Tales of Old Japan*, by A.B. Mitford [1871]. It's also posted online at www.sarudama.com/japanesefolklore_vampirecat.shtml.)

Despite the apparent risks, oriental cats were kept for their hunting ability and their beauty. When cats were introduced to Japan sometime between the eighth and tenth centuries, they were first kept as exotic pets that only the wealthy could afford, but they soon began to earn their keep. Silk was one of Japan's most important industries, and mice were eating the silk worms, as well as the grain stores. Cats were the solution to both problems.

Oriental cats were also believed to bring luck. An old Buddhist superstition says that there will be silver in the house of a light cat, gold in the house of a dark one. The belief in cats as agents of luck and prosperity can still be seen in Japan in the Maneki Neko, or the Beckoning Cat, a white cat with a raised paw that's displayed in many business establishments. There are at least three legends of how the Maneki Neko came into being, and all of them involve cats that brought luck or protection to their owners; one cat even killed a snake to save its geisha-mistress *after* the cat was beheaded. (You can find some of these legends at www.en.wikipedia.org/wiki/Maneki_Neko.)

All of which brings us, finally, to the cats of the House of Night series.

## THE CATS OF THE HOUSE OF NIGHT

"Cats choose us; we don't own them."

—*Marked*

The cats of the House of Night resonate with all of these traditions, but—though they are never referred to as such—their role is most like that of the familiar. Familiars are usually associated with witches, and vampyres aren't exactly witches, though their worship of the Goddess and their rituals are very closely aligned with Pagan and Wiccan beliefs. The whole time I was reading the books, I couldn't help thinking how much these cats were like familiars. And in *The Fledgling Handbook 101*, the ritual for saying good-bye to a deceased cat is called "Release of a Familiar." But, as with the other mythical influences in the series, the idea of cats as familiars has been creatively modified to fit with the House of Night universe.

Familiars are exactly what their name implies—creatures who are familiar to you, as if, long before you first meet, you already know each other. Cats that are familiars are attuned to you on a psychic, possibly magical, level. It's as if you and the cat are friends for all time, before this lifetime, in this lifetime, and in lifetimes still to come. The Casts nail this perfectly.

In *Marked*, before Zoey and Nala find each other, Zoey dreams of a little orange tabby who's yelling at her in an old lady's voice, asking what had taken her so long to get there. Then, when Zoey meets Nala—or, more precisely, when Nala finds her—Zoey recognizes the cat from her dream. They are already familiar to each other, because they share a psychic link.

Many people who have cats will tell you that cats are exquisitely tuned to their humans' emotions, comforting their owners when they're upset, making them laugh when they're blue, giving them reproachful looks when they're not doing what they should. Nala fits all of this to a tee. She's the one who's always there to comfort Zoey. After Zoey first drinks her first drop of Heath's blood and is badly shaken by how much she craves it, Nala materializes and presses her face against Zoey's wet cheek. After Zoey realizes that Loren and Neferet are lovers and that she, Zoey, has been set up and played for a fool, she runs to the old oak tree where she breaks down crying. Unsurprisingly, it's Nala who appears, wet nose poking against Zoey's cheek, putting a paw on her shoulder and "purring furiously." Nala, who loves Zoey unconditionally, is the only one whom Zoey can tell just how badly she messed up. Later, as Zoey is reviewing all the pluses and minus in her life, Nala jumps into her arms to comfort her—and sneezes directly into Zoey's face, giving Zoey a great last line for the book: "As usual, Nala summed up my life perfectly: kinda funny, kinda gross, and more than kinda messy" (*Chosen*).

To which I'd add, "And kinda magical." Because even now the idea of a familiar goes far beyond pet and companion. Today, there are many people who openly practice Wiccan and Pagan rituals, and many of them consider their cats to be their familiars—equals who help perform magic and spells. Marion Weinstein (1939–2009), who was a priestess and a practicing witch in New York City, explained that cats make wonderful companions for witches because they're not afraid of the unseen world or spirits, and they're very good at knowing when the spirits are present and will often welcome them into a ceremony, making the witch's task easier. Cats are also good at psychic work, able to communicate directly with their human, mind-to-mind.

Many cultures have believed cats could perceive things invisible to humans and even see into the future. As Van Vechten writes (in *The Tiger in the House*), people in the East "are aware that this animal wavers on the borderland between the natural and the supernatural, the conscious and the subconscious"—a description that makes me think of the vampyres, who are of the human world and also worlds beyond it. So it seems quite fitting that their chosen companions are cats, which also share this ability to walk in two worlds. And though the House of Night cats don't turn into people or ghosts—at least not in the first seven books—their ability to perceive the supernatural realm allows them to warn their people of danger.

It's easiest to see this in Nala, who, long before Stark becomes Zoey's Warrior, is Zoey's protector. When the first two dead fledglings reappear, it's Nala who sees them first—who sees into the realm of the supernatural and perceives what Zoey's still mostly human eyes can't. Nala sees Elizabeth, the first of the undead vamps, and immediately hisses and spits. She even attacks Elliot, fighting to protect Zoey. It's Nala launching herself at Elliot that makes Zoey realize that she's not seeing a ghost; that these dead fledglings are somehow not dead. Even though Nala knows Stevie Rae well, when Stevie Rae returns from the dead, Nala yowls and spits and starts to hurl herself at her, which should warn Zoey that maybe this new incarnation of Stevie Rae is not completely trustworthy. Nala even seems to understand that Kalona is able to enter Zoey's dreams. After dreaming of the fallen angel, Zoey wakes to find Nala growling at his dream presence. There's no doubt that Nala can see into the spirit world.

As for the House of Night cats seeing the future, there's that very cool moment in *Marked* when, soon after Nala finds her, Zoey returns to her room and essentially finds a cat starter kit, complete with cat food, litter box, litter, and a little pink collar. When Zoey asks Stevie Rae where the gift came from, Stevie Rae hands her a note. It reads: *"Skylar told me she was coming.* It was signed with a single letter: N." In this case, not only does Skylar, Neferet's cat, know that Nala has found and will move in with Zoey, but he's able to communicate this to Neferet, who has an affinity for cats.

One thing I love about the cats in House of Night is that though the Casts clearly adore cats, they don't sentimentalize them. These cats are not perfect mythic goddesses. Rather, Nala is often described as grumpy and complaining at

Zoey like an old woman, and she is forever sneezing in Zoey's face. Maleficent, the bad-tempered Persian Aphrodite rescues from Street Cats in *Untamed*, is often described by Zoey as Aphrodite's snobby, "furry clone." Beelzebub, the suitably named sleek gray cat who shares the "twins," Shaunie and Erin, is forever chasing and terrorizing the other House of Night felines. The Casts know that cats are as individual as we are, and some of them have bad moods, wicked tempers, and a talent for holding grudges.

But the cats always come through, warning their vampyres of danger, even gathering together in Zoey's room to let her know who her allies are. When Kalona and Neferet take over the House of Night and most of its population, Zoey finds Dragon Lankford's Maine Coon and Professor Lenobia's Siamese in her room and knows that the two professors can be trusted. The cats even provide a surprisingly coordinated distraction so that Jack can sit with Stark's body in the morgue. When Zoey and her friends leave campus to stay in the tunnels with the red vampyres, the cats accompany them. And in one of the most touching scenes of the series, when Dragon sits by the funeral pyre for his wife, Anastasia, he has to stop Anastasia's grieving white cat from hurling itself into the fire.

Cats seem to touch us on a deep, subconscious level. We have worshipped them as gods and burned them as witches. We have considered them symbols of healing and fertility, as well as incarnations of Satan. We've even convinced ourselves that they're responsible for good and bad luck. Honestly, if you read enough cat lore what you get is that humans are capable of believing just about anything about any creature. We have a bizarre ability to demonize or deify, and cats have been the objects of our best and worst impulses. And yet, through all the human extremes, cats have remained very much the same, true to themselves and their own unique, inscrutable nature.

The seventh book of the House of Night series, *Burned*, is oddly catless. This is because Zoey and her friends travel to Venice and beyond and simply can't take the cats with them. I enjoyed the book completely. It's a terrific story that draws on Celtic folklore and is quite different from all the others in the series. But much as I love it, I missed the cats.

## *Great Books on Cat Lore*

*Nine Lives: The Folklore of Cats,* by Katherine M. Briggs
*The Cult of the Cat,* by Patricia Dale Green.
*Cat Catalog: The Ultimate Cat Book,* by Judy Fireman, ed.
*The Tribe of Tiger: Cats and Their Culture,* by Elizabeth Marshall Thomas
*The Tiger in the House: The Classic Book on the History, Manners and Habits of the Cat,* by Carl Van Vechten

Though most of these are older books, you can still find them easily at libraries or on used-book websites like www.abebooks.com. And a great collection of cat sayings can be found at www.catquotes.com/catquotes.htm.

ELLEN STEIBER is a writer and editor who lives in Tucson, Arizona, where she shares a house with her husband and Catalina, a very beautiful and mischievous tortoiseshell cat. Catalina, they all agree, runs the house. Ellen has written essays in *A New Dawn, Demigods and Monsters,* and *The World of the Golden Compass,* as well as the novel *A Rumor of Gems.* She is currently working on the sequel to the novel as well as a young adult novel. The young adult novel is set in Tucson and involves teenage girls, horses, and several very tricksy cats.

# { Reimagining "Magic City" }

## HOW THE CASTS MYTHOLOGIZE TULSA

*Amy H. Sturgis*

MY OWN journey to the House of Night began with an email from my little sister, Margret. She explained that I should read—no, had to read—the novels by P.C. and Kristin Cast. While I appreciated her recommendation, I wasn't exactly in the market for new titles to enjoy. My "to read" stack already was well out of hand.

Then Margret changed my mind with one simple sentence: "The books are set in Tulsa."

The next thing I knew, I was reading the opening scene of the first book, in which a vampyre Tracker Marks Zoey Montgomery in the hall of her school and my alma mater, South Intermediate High School, in the Tulsa suburb of Broken Arrow. I was hooked.

Of course, familiarity has its own charm. Like Zoey, I've shopped at Utica Square, trusted meteorologist Travis Meyer for the day's weather forecast, and even taken a science class from Mr. Wise, and this helped me to feel an immediate identification with the young fledgling. As I've read the series, I've enjoyed many an inside joke that no doubt qualifies as a "Tulsa thing," from the similarity between Aphrodite's father, Mayor LaFont, and Tulsa's former mayor, William "Bill" LaFortune, to the ever-present digs at Broken Arrow's main rival, Union. (Go Tigers!) As someone who grew up in Tulsa but now lives many miles away, I've appreciated how the novels can be read together as one extended and creative love letter to my hometown.

But the Casts have accomplished far more than giving former and current Tulsans a collective, cozy feeling of home. Certainly a number of contemporary series—including other young adult vampire series—use real-world locations for their settings. What sets the Casts' House of Night novels apart is how the authors have harnessed the preexisting history and folklore of Tulsa, from its architecture to its ghost stories, to mythologize the town. In the first decades of the twentieth century, Tulsa was known as "Magic City" thanks to its oil boom and the immediate wealth it provided; today, P.C. and Kristin Cast have transformed Tulsa with their own equally rich form of magic.

## TULSA AS A CHARACTER

In effect, the Casts make their reimagined Tulsa a character in its own right in the House of Night novels, and this marks their series as a contemporary example of a time-honored literary tradition: the Gothic romance. When Horace Walpole put ink to paper in 1764 and produced *The Castle of Otranto*, he created not only a genre, but also many of the rules it would follow, and soon the Gothic tradition that he pioneered gave birth to vampire fiction with works such as "The Vampyre" (1819) by John Polidori and "The Skeleton Count," or "The Vampire Mistress" (1828) by Elizabeth Caroline Grey. As Jerrold E. Hogle points out in *The Cambridge Companion to Gothic Fiction*, Gothic works blur the line between the natural and the supernatural. They also deal with secrets (that are either physically or psychologically haunting), focus on the past (either the past in general or a personal, recent past), and remain deeply rooted in their geographical settings.

As writers in the Gothic tradition, P.C. and Kristin Cast understand this well. They blur the line between the natural and supernatural routinely, as I first discovered when I read of a vampyre Tracker in my former high school. By steeping their novels in Tulsa and its folklore, the Casts also use local weather, tragic history, and notable landmarks in the city to evoke haunting secrets, provide a sense of the past, and allow readers to connect with their stories in a stirring, visceral way.

Certainly the authors have used Tulsa's local weather to powerful effect. Perhaps the most striking example of this is the ice storm that features heavily in the events of the fifth and sixth novels, *Hunted* and *Tempted*. In these books, the storm heightens the characters' sense of helplessness and isolation during dire events and hampers their ability to move, building dramatic tension. Tulsa's loss of electricity due to the storm leaves the city paralyzed in darkness, appropriately symbolizing how Neferet and her new partner, the immortal Kalona, have unleashed evil on the town in their bid for personal power. P.C. noted in her blog that she and her daughter modeled their descriptions on the real ice storm that crippled Tulsa in December 2007. I doubt the storm would have seemed as authentic or eerie if the Casts hadn't drawn on their firsthand memories of the event, and I can imagine that Tulsan readers of the House of Night series relived their own struggles with the storm while reading about the plight of Zoey and her friends.

The Casts also tap into the power of local history. One of the most memorable examples of this, to my mind, occurs in the second book of the series, *Betrayed*. When Zoey tries to explain her plan for involving the fledglings of the Dark Daughters and Sons in charity work in the local community, the House of Night's High Priestess Neferet reminds her of the power of human fear and hatred toward vampyres. To explain the danger of prejudice Neferet might easily have called upon trite illustrations made bland by time, distance, and overuse. Instead, she refers to an event that is all too recent and painful in Tulsa memory: the Greenwood riots, also known as the Tulsa race riots.

From May 31 to June 1, 1921, a group of white Tulsans burned nearly thirty-five city blocks in Greenwood, the African-American section of town, utterly destroying the prosperous area known as "Black Wall Street." This left approximately 10,000 black Tulsans homeless and an unknown number dead. According to Scott Ellsworth's lauded history *Death in a Promised*

*Land: The Tulsa Race Riot of 1921*, the Greenwood riots represent one of the single most devastating moments of racial violence in a century of U.S. history. Today Tulsans of all races continue to consider and wrestle with the legacy of this tragedy. Thus when Neferet says, "Those African-American humans were part of Tulsa, and Tulsa destroyed them," her words resonate deeply, because they refer to a very real and violent example from Tulsans' very own backyard.

Fortunately, as Zoey points out, "it's not 1920 anymore." However, the Casts make it clear that prejudice is not simply a problem of the past. Tension between the human and vampyre populations boils just beneath the surface of their reimagined Tulsa, threatening to spill over violently at any moment. Perhaps more to the point, this prejudice represents a tool that can be used by unscrupulous leaders of both populations. Neferet herself later plays upon vampyres' and humans' hatred toward each other as she builds her own base of power, illustrating how a people's prejudices can make them easily led— and misled. The insight and seriousness with which the authors deal with the ongoing issues of fear and hatred suggest that they keep the lessons of Tulsa's history close to heart as they craft their novels.

## NOTABLE LANDMARKS

By incorporating recent weather and local history into their fiction, the Casts create a firm setting for the House of Night series, a Tulsa that feels three-dimensional, well grounded, and authentic. Then they take their literary game to yet another level by anchoring their stories to specific, real-world Tulsa landmarks. These locations come ready-made with their own mystique and folklore attached. In true Gothic style, the Casts enlist the city's most remarkable places in the cause of their fiction, constructing new stories upon the mysteries and legends retold and refined by generations of Tulsans. The Casts' mythologized Tulsa is so compelling, I would argue, because it springs from such deep-rooted sources. Obviously you don't have to know the ins and outs of Tulsa firsthand in order to enjoy the House of Night series, but you can gain a greater appreciation of the Casts' artistry if you consider the creative ways in which they employ the city's notable sites.

## Cascia Hall

Of course many of the settings featured in the novels, from the friendly Street Cats rescue to the tranquil Mary's Grotto, do exist in Tulsa today. But the Casts reserve their most fantastic and intense action for some of Tulsa's most atmospheric spots. One of these is Cascia Hall, the elite Catholic college preparatory school whose campus becomes Tulsa's House of Night.

It's not difficult to see why the Casts chose Cascia Hall as the setting for their vampyre finishing school. At the heart of the Cascia Hall complex sits the original monastery, which dates back to the school's founding by the Order of Saint Augustine in 1926. Even the newer constructions follow the same neo-French Norman style of architecture, thus lending an atmosphere of Old World history and gravity to a campus not yet a century old. The founders named the school for Saint Rita of Cascia, Italy, and the imposing Saint Rita of Cascia Chapel occupies a key position on its grounds. In the Casts' novels, this becomes Nyx's Temple at the House of Night.

Cascia Hall's appearance sets it apart from the rest of Tulsa. First, its castle-like buildings and towers differ from the other noteworthy constructions in the region; in fact, they look positively medieval, as if they predate the rest of the city and state. (Thus Zoey, during her first tour of the grounds in *Marked*, thinks to herself, "I swear, a moat would have looked more like it belonged there than a sidewalk . . .") Second, the forty wooded acres of the campus divide it from the residential neighborhood in which it sits. Although entrances to Cascia Hall exist on both South Yorktown Avenue and South Utica Avenue, the South Utica entrance remains closed except during athletic events. The school thus appears to be as exclusive geographically and architecturally as it is academically and financially. To mainstream Tulsans, this isolation lends the place a certain (dare I say Gothic?) mystery. Tucked away, secretive, and utterly distinctive, the campus offers the perfect home for the supernatural or paranormal—in short, for the Casts' vampyres.

## The Philbrook Museum of Art

Together the Philbrook Museum of Art and its grounds seem to have emerged directly from a book of classic legends. As a very young child, I accompanied my parents to an outdoor evening showing of *Camelot* on the Philbrook's manicured lawn, and I recall that it was difficult to tell where the fictional kingdom of Camelot ended and the real grounds of the Philbrook began.

Waite Phillips, I think, would've been delighted at this. One of three brothers who made their fortunes from Oklahoma oil, Waite Phillips (1883–1964) wanted his seventy-two room home and its twenty-three acre surroundings to seem like a piece of Italian history transplanted to contemporary Tulsa. Completed in 1927, Villa Philbrook is a masterpiece of Italian Renaissance design. Its elaborate gardens mimic those created by Giacomo Barozzi da Vignola for the Villa Lante in 1566, following the Mannerist style of the Italian High Renaissance long appreciated for its intellectual sophistication and symmetry rather than its naturalism. The gardens, like the villa itself, reflect conscious craftsmanship and delicate artistry.

It's easy to understand why Aphrodite chooses the domed gazebo at the foot of the garden for her Samhain ritual in *Marked*. After all, there could hardly be a more dramatic setting for a drama queen. Technically, the "gazebo" is a tempietto, a circular Renaissance temple, and it serves as the focal point of interest from the Villa Philbrook's back terrace. The museum's garden and paved walks all point directly to the structure, and the small pool before it reflects back the image of its long white columns. As readers discover, Aphrodite's ritual for the Dark Daughters and Sons goes badly wrong there, and in the aftermath the Philbrook gazebo becomes the setting for Zoey Redbird's unplanned debut as a future High Priestess. It seems appropriate that Zoey finds herself, in her words, in a setting like "a magical fairy kingdom" when taking her first steps as a leader specially chosen by her Goddess.

The Casts return repeatedly to the remarkable location of the Philbrook Museum to further the plots of their novels. In *Betrayed*, for example, police find the mangled body of Union football player Brad Higeons in a stream on the Philbrook grounds. In *Chosen*, Zoey picks the Philbrook gazebo as the place to reunite with her once dead and now drastically altered best friend, Stevie Rae. Never does the Philbrook appear to be a threatening place in its own right; the only concern any of the characters seem to feel is that of attracting the attention of human security guards after museum hours, and this rates more as an inconvenience than a threat. Instead, the sheer exoticism of the place seems to heighten already powerful emotions, from dread and terror to joy and triumph.

This fits well with the reputation the Philbrook enjoys among Tulsans. After an apparently happy tenure in Villa Philbrook, Waite Phillips donated his home to the city in 1938 as a showcase for his eclectic and extensive art collection. The museum opened in 1939. No guidebook or ghost tour marks the Philbrook as a "haunted" place, and yet a quick Google search will reveal half a dozen Tulsa-based blogs that report vague, unusual happenings there: painted portraits whose eyes follow visitors, for instance, or outdoor sculptures that turn their heads to watch passersby. None of the accounts suggests anything malevolent or unwelcoming—or even particularly specific. But it seems that some Tulsans want to think of the Philbrook as too grand, too spectacular to be contained by the natural, normal laws of the everyday world. In short, it's an ideal spot for the Casts to use in their supernatural, paranormal reimagining of Tulsa.

## The Union Depot

Another key Tulsa landmark that appears often in the House of Night series is the Union Depot. This heavyset, imposing structure offers a contrary note to the architectural chorus of downtown Tulsa. Some of the surrounding buildings sprang up in the oil boom days of the 1920s and reflect the extravagance of that time, from the Gothic Philtower, complete with leering gargoyles, to the elegant Philcade building, adorned with wrought-iron embellishments. (Both buildings were named for Waite Phillips.) A number of the structures reflect early art deco sensibilities—so many, in fact, that Tulsa once was called "Terra Cotta City" because of the terra cotta art deco tiles carved in geometric and zigzag patterns that grace both the exteriors and interiors of the buildings. Even today, travel guides such as 2010's *Insiders' Guide to Tulsa* by Elaine Warner include special art deco tours of downtown Tulsa.

After the Stock Market Crash of 1929, however, architectural tastes changed. The Tulsa Union Depot was built in 1931 and represents what's known as the PWA (Public Works Administration) art deco style. Its solemn lines project calm stability, almost severity, rather than flashy extravagance, but the design still boasts the classic art deco zigzag pattern. The sheer scale of the structure certainly suggests permanence, and the size was needed, for in its heyday the Union Depot served three separate railroads and their passengers.

After closing its doors in 1967, the proud building sat empty and deserted for years. Looters stripped its interior, and the deteriorating roof collapsed.

Here the Casts' version of Tulsa diverges from actual Tulsa history. Today the Union Depot, fully renovated, houses the impressive Oklahoma Jazz Hall of Fame and the Tulsa Symphony Orchestra. In the House of Night series, however, the depot remains empty and forlorn. In Zoey's words from *Betrayed*, "It looked like something that should be in the Gotham City of the Batman Dark Knight comics." Stevie Rae describes it in *Tempted* as having a "*Blade Runner* meets *Amityville Horror*" look.

The Casts accomplish several things by reimagining the Union Depot in this way. First and foremost, the idea of that elegant yet austere building sitting dark and ravaged is downright spooky. Not many people would be lining up to take a midnight tour, I can assure you. The city might be too young to boast the ageless, windswept moors of *Wuthering Heights* or the legendary castle of *Dracula*, but this depiction of the depot adds to the notion of Tulsa—especially Tulsa at night—as an old, forbidding, haunted place straight out of a classic Gothic romance.

The authors' choice also enhances the story line most closely linked to the Union Depot in the novels, that of the self-imposed exile of the red vampyres who live beneath it. The abandoned depot represents something dead, decayed, and absolutely wrong, which is exactly how readers first view the once deceased and now transformed red fledglings. This Gothic sense of wrongness is doubly potent for Tulsa readers, who recognize that the depot isn't in this dire condition in "real life." The disturbing unnaturalness of the neglected depot mirrors the disturbing unnaturalness of these vamps, their origins, and their dark appetites.

Last, leaving the Union Depot abandoned frees the space to be used for events in the books. The most spine-chilling action there occurs in the fifth novel of the series, *Hunted*, when the leader of the rogue red vampyres, Nicole, and her followers trap Stevie Rae on the roof and leave her to burn to death in the morning sun. Rephaim, the Raven Mocker who owes Stevie Rae his life, saves her. The dark towers and intimidating lines of the depot roof offer the perfect backdrop for the dramatic betrayal, near murder, and remarkable rescue.

These events couldn't have taken place if the Casts had used the current restored depot instead. Even if the Oklahoma Jazz Hall of Fame and Tulsa

Symphony Orchestra employees and visitors somehow had remained oblivious to red vampyres living in the tunnels below them, and vampyre fledglings using their toilets and showers, I'm guessing they would have noticed a red vampyre High Priestess smoking on the rooftop and a Raven Mocker climbing in the trees. By emptying the Union Depot, the Casts open it up to their alternate universe and the tales it contains.

## The Tulsa Tunnels

Beneath the buildings of downtown lies one of the most fascinating features of the real Tulsa landscape, a complex system of underground tunnels. Local legend has it that these tunnels were created to move alcohol during Prohibition, which began nationwide in 1920 and continued in Tulsa until 1957. I remember hearing these stories, and so does Heath Luck, Zoey's on-again, off-again human boyfriend/consort. I have no doubt that the tunnels did prove very handy to bootleggers at various times in Tulsa's history, but they actually had their origin in a different and more legitimate cause. Apparently construction began on the tunnels in the early 1930s to move freight between some of Tulsa's businesses. According to Alice Froeschle, owner of Bandana Tours, Waite Phillips (the same millionaire who built Villa Philbrook) soon adapted them for his own purposes.

It seems that in the 1930s, Phillips began to feel a bit nervous about walking the streets of Tulsa unprotected. This might sound rather paranoid, but considering the events of his day, it's understandable. In 1932, the baby son of wealthy aviator Charles Lindbergh was kidnapped from his home in New Jersey, and even though the Lindberghs paid ransom, the infant was murdered. Somewhat closer to home, notorious criminal George "Machine Gun" Kelly abducted the wealthy Oklahoma City oilman Charles F. Urschel from his home in 1933. Kelly held Urschel hostage until he received a ransom payment. Waite Phillips did not want to become the next victim in the headlines of national newspapers. He felt more secure knowing that he and his colleagues and loved ones could walk from one place of business to another using private routes below the city streets, and thus had the Tulsa tunnel system expanded.

The tunnels both in reality and in Tulsa folklore differ from those described in the House of Night series, but not as much as one might think. It's true that the tunnel system is less extensive in the real Tulsa than in the city reimagined by the Casts. Visitors to the Union Depot today, for example, will find clean, bright pedestrian bridges for their convenience rather than rusted gratings leading down to shadowy subterranean passages. Furthermore, many of the tunnels that do exist and remain open are in excellent repair. Well lit and decorated, these tunnels are used by Tulsa professionals as part of their daily routines.

But enough mystery—and, let's face it, creepiness—surrounds the tunnels to make them excellent tools in the Casts' mythologizing of Tulsa. When downtown public relations professional Andrea Myers led a guest tour for readers of the *Tasha Does Tulsa* blog on February 22, 2010, she admitted that some portions of the tunnels remain dank and wet to this day, with rotting ceiling tiles dripping water into buckets. She also noted that random doors appear in the tunnels without signs to identify them, doors that seem "to not have been opened for decades." Legends feed on such things.

Teri French, the founder of Tulsa Spirit Tours, relates in her 2010 book, *Tulsa's Haunted Memories*, several fantastic stories linked to downtown Tulsa tunnels and drainage systems. According to French, traditional tales about the Tulsa underground include rumors of satanic rituals, animal sacrifice, and other occult activity. One repeated story tells of the discovery of a temporary shrine to the ancient goddess Isis that allegedly appeared one day and disappeared the next. Although such rumors remain unsubstantiated, they refuse to die. All of the tales agree that strange people may be involved in dark deeds beneath the downtown streets of Tulsa.

The Casts harness both the real and the folkloric elements of the tunnels to craft their mythology. The tunnels first appear in the second book of the series, *Betrayed*, and they play an important role in all of the subsequent novels to date. When readers initially encounter them, they serve as the dark lair of the sinister red vampyres who have captured and tormented Heath and are preparing to kill him. In Heath's words, the tunnels are "more like caves… They're dark and wet and disgusting." Zoey's experience there confirms the reader's opinion: the tunnels are bad news, peopled with frightening creatures and dangerous to anyone who ventures into them.

Over time, however, the reader's understanding of the tunnels evolves just as Zoey's does. When Stevie Rae regains her humanity and becomes the High

Priestess of the red vampyres, the tunnels change outwardly to echo her inner transformation. They become a sanctuary to Stevie Rae and her followers, with comfortable individual bedrooms and homey touches—not to mention some high-end interior decorating thanks to Aphrodite's credit cards. The red vampyres feel most secure underground, and Stevie Rae draws special strength from there, as well, thanks to her Goddess-given earth affinity. Zoey and her friends even find the tunnels a source of refuge at the end of *Untamed* and remain there during part of *Hunted*. When the tunnels become contested ground in *Burned*, readers appreciate how much is at stake, and Stevie Rae's ultimate victory there brings with it a poignant relief.

Whether the source of whispered stories or the stuff of everyday routine, the tunnels under downtown Tulsa have played an important role in the city for nearly eighty years. Just as Tulsans find the tunnels a source of both fear and protection, so the Casts use the tunnels alternately to represent threat and safety.

## The Gilcrease Museum and Home

Arguably the most noteworthy Tulsa landmark that the Casts feature in their books, at least in terms of local legend and folklore, appears later in the House of Night series: the Gilcrease Museum and its grounds are not mentioned until the end of the sixth novel, *Tempted*. Stevie Rae decides that the mansion on the museum property is the perfect place for Rephaim to hide while recovering from his injuries. As she explains, the Gilcrease mansion's reputation ensures that Rephaim won't be discovered or disturbed: "And here's the best part—it's super haunted! . . . so if someone sees or hears something weird—meaning you—they'll freak and think it's just more ghost stuff."

Most Tulsans, I think, would agree with Stevie Rae's logic. While the Gilcrease Museum is famous for housing one of the world's most impressive collections of artwork and artifacts related to the American West, the Gilcrease Museum grounds are infamous for altogether different reasons.

Thomas Gilcrease (1890–1962) became a multimillionaire when oil was discovered on the land allotment he received as a member of the Creek Nation. While in his early twenties, he grew enamored with a mansion he saw being built of native sandstone from the Osage Hills in west Tulsa, and he bought the home and the eighty acres surrounding it. This became known as the House on the Hill, or Tom's House. He later built a second structure on his property to serve as a museum, and in 1949, the Thomas Gilcrease Institute of American History and Art opened.

For many years Gilcrease found success and fame as a businessman, philanthropist, and collector, but he failed to find domestic happiness. His first marriage to the Osage sweetheart of his teens ended after sixteen years; his second marriage, to a nineteen-year-old Cherokee Tulsan and Miss America, lasted less than six. While Gilcrease traveled the world in the 1940s, his home became an orphanage for Native American children. Gilcrease later returned to live in Tom's House, and in 1962, he suffered a fatal heart attack there and was buried in a mausoleum nearby. Today the grounds of the Gilcrease Museum consist of the museum itself, the Gilcrease mansion and mausoleum, and 460 acres of land, including twenty-three acres of themed gardens designed to complement the museum's collections.

According to Tulsa tradition, Thomas Gilcrease still walks his property. The Gilcrease Museum therefore remains a staple for area ghost tours. In *Tulsa's Haunted Memories*, Teri French relates multiple cases of supposed sightings of Gilcrease in the museum, the gardens, and the mansion. She suggests that Gilcrease's ongoing appearances may explain the supposedly notorious turnover rate among the property's night staff.

Tom's House, in particular, continues to capture the imagination of Tulsans. In the House of Night series, the Gilcrease home, like the Union Depot, sits deserted. In Tulsa today, the mansion is empty but in reasonable repair, and visitors may tour certain rooms. If the Casts have altered its condition somewhat for the purposes of their plot—it would, after all, have been more difficult for Rephaim to go unnoticed if museum patrons were touring his hideout—they nevertheless stick closely to Tulsa folklore regarding the mansion's unearthly occupants. Just as Stevie Rae claimed, the house itself does have the reputation of being one of the most haunted buildings in Tulsa.

In April and May 2002, the Paranormal Investigation Team of Tulsa (PITT) conducted two publicized investigations of the mansion assisted by the Oklahoma City Ghost Club. According to both organizations' websites, the team members drew similar conclusions based on their experiences as well as the readings and recordings they gathered. These conclusions agree with the legends that say Thomas Gilcrease isn't alone in visiting his home. The investigators claim that the spirits of several children also remain in the house, quite likely the ghosts of youngsters who lived there when it was an orphanage in the 1940s. Some of the footage from this investigation ran on local news channel FOX23, reinforcing and rekindling the stories surrounding the site.

P.C. and Kristin build directly on the reputation of the Gilcrease mansion. In *Burned*, the authors make their boldest and most imaginative move in mythologizing Tulsa: they allow their fictional character Rephaim to interact directly with a spirit straight out of Tulsa legend, one of the several unnamed child ghosts from the Gilcrease mansion. While Rephaim lies low in the house, the spirit of a little girl appears to him, asking him questions about his identity.

This sequence becomes even more compelling after one reads the rest of the novel, especially if the reader knows the history of the Gilcrease home. Later in *Burned*, the reader glimpses Rephaim in his human, Native American incarnation (which is appropriate, since Raven Mockers come from Cherokee mythology), but this occurs only after the ghost of the little girl has made him question what he really is. If the girl hails from the Gilcrease mansion's orphanage days, it follows that she, too, is Native American, and quite possibly Cherokee. In short, the Casts use the legend surrounding the Gilcrease home as a means to bring two mythic symbols of the Native American past—the Raven Mocker and the ghost—into dialogue with each other in the present. They turn Tulsa folklore into a canonical part of their own fiction, just as they do with older myth and legend.

## HOUSE OF NIGHT TOURS

The incorporation of Tulsa landmarks and their corresponding legends lends a rich authenticity and texture to the Casts' books. In turn, the terrific success of the bestselling House of Night series means that many people are discovering Tulsa either for the first time or in a new way. As I write this, the publisher of the novels, St. Martin's Press, is collaborating with the Tulsa Chamber of Commerce and the Oklahoma Tourism Department to develop two innovative ways for readers to experience the Tulsa sites reimagined by the Casts.

First, the publisher intends to offer a onetime tour of Tulsa locations for the lucky winners of a House of Night-themed sweepstakes corresponding roughly with the January 2011 debut of the eighth book in the series, *Awakened*. Second, St. Martin's plans to provide through its website a virtual tour that will serve not only as a long-distance interactive experience of Tulsa, but also as a checklist for those who wish to go on self-guided tours of the city in person. This virtual tour is scheduled to go live in Spring 2011, and remain online for the foreseeable future to complement the final novels in the series—so you may be able to check it out for yourself right now. Both tours will incorporate sites such as the Philbrook Museum, the Tulsa tunnels, and the Union Depot. Needless to say, these tours seem like promising ways to encourage tourism and exploration of Tulsa, as well as promote the House of Night novels. Many of the local businesses that are mentioned in the novels, from the Street Cats charity to the Utica Square shopping center to the Little Black Dress boutique, are actively helping to bring the tour plans to life.

Not everyone, however, seems as happy as I am that the House of Night series is turning new attention to Tulsa. Representatives of Cascia Hall have elected not to cooperate with the book-related Tulsa tours. From this I infer that some Cascia Hall officials, at least, don't appreciate the way in which their institution is portrayed in the novels.

To be fair, Cascia Hall does not receive terrific praise from the Casts. In *Marked*, Neferet tells Zoey that the House of Night purchased its campus five years earlier from Cascia Hall after making the "arrogant headmaster an offer even he couldn't refuse." Zoey recognizes that this purchase came after "a whole herd of kids who went to Cascia Hall had been busted for drugs." Of course, the Casts don't portray any school body as perfect; even sympathetic Broken Arrow students such as Heath are shown to abuse alcohol and smoke marijuana. But in Zoey's mind, at least, the memory of Cascia Hall seems synonymous with stuck-up rich kids behaving badly. Meanwhile the forbidding buildings of the campus, although exotic and elegant, appear to Zoey "like something out of a creepy dream."

Perhaps it's also worth noting that early on in *Marked* the authors link Cascia Hall by name with the People of Faith rather than with the Tulsa

Catholic community, despite the school's Catholic affiliation. This may be significant because, throughout the novels, the People of Faith are often depicted as judgmental, dogmatic, and hypocritical, not to mention patriarchal in practice. (Note that Neferet refers to the headmaster at Cascia Hall as a "he.") In contrast, specific Catholic organizations such as the Street Cats rescue and the Benedictine Abbey are often depicted as tolerant, generous, and humanitarian, represented by powerful feminine forces (various nuns and the Virgin Mary herself). This subtly suggests that the leadership at Cascia Hall demonstrates more of the negative qualities that the Casts identify in contemporary Christianity than the positive ones.

In other words, the House of Night series won't be used as promotional literature for Cascia Hall anytime soon. (I for one won't be staying up nights worrying about the school's enrollment figures.) Nevertheless, the tours offer school representatives the chance to show Cascia Hall in its best light and employ the House of Night-generated publicity for their institution's advantage. If its leaders do not choose to take advantage of this, that's a shame.

## ENJOY YOUR STAY

While the Cascia Hall leadership may not embrace the attention brought by the House of Night series, other Tulsans and former Tulsans, myself included, will continue to celebrate the creative manner in which P.C. and Kristin mythologize Tulsa in their fiction. Thanks to widespread interest in their bestselling books, others worldwide will come to know and appreciate the city, as well. As Tulsa enriches the House of Night novels, it also is enriched by them, and will continue to be for many years to come.

Perhaps the saying is correct, and you really can't go home again. These days when I return to Tulsa, whether in body or just in spirit, I see a vampyre fledgling here and a Raven Mocker there in places I hadn't found them years ago. That's fine by me. Through this new lens the town appears larger than life and mythological in proportion, but it's also true to itself in every way that's meaningful.

P.C. and Kristin Cast have made Tulsa once again the "Magic City," and I heart them for that.

AMY H. STURGIS earned her PhD in intellectual history at Vanderbilt University. A specialist in science fiction/fantasy studies and Native American studies, Sturgis is the author of four books and the editor of another five. Her essays have appeared in dozens of books, journals, and magazines. In 2006, she was honored with the Imperishable Flame Award for J.R.R. Tolkien Scholarship. In 2009, she received the Sofanaut Award for her regular "History of the Genre" segments on *StarShipSofa*, which in 2010 became the first podcast in history to win a Hugo Award. Her official website is amyhsturgis.com.

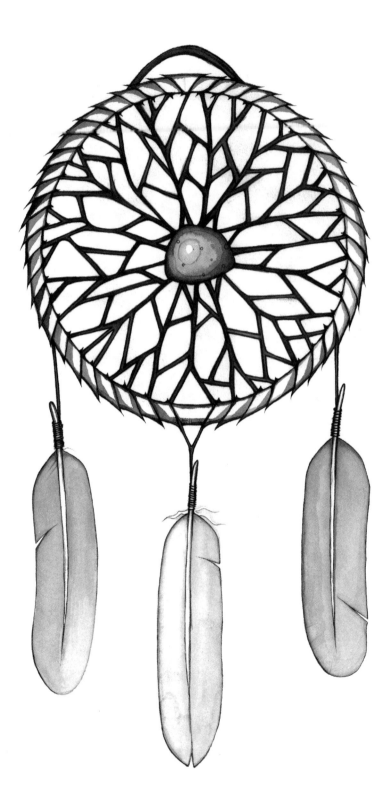

# The Magic of Being Cherokee

*Jordan Dane*

THE HOUSE of Night series is unique from other vampyre lore in many ways, but when authors P. C. and Kristin Cast add depth to the fictional character of Zoey Redbird by giving her the Native American blood of a Cherokee, that's where the magic in these novels becomes truly special. Native American culture is used as a springboard for the fictional world depicted in the series. The authors research real Cherokee myths and legends to add color and authenticity, then add creative twists to bring these myths alive on the page. And although the authors have never claimed to be experts on the Cherokee, the strength and depth of the Cherokee Nation shines like a beacon through their young heroine.

Sixteen-year-old Zoey Redbird is from Broken Arrow, Oklahoma. Though Oklahoma is home to a larger-than-average Cherokee population, Zoey's Cherokee roots still mean she looks different from the other kids at her school: with her black hair, olive-toned skin, high cheekbones, and large, captivating hazel eyes, she stands out in the crowd. In *Marked*, after she's branded with the outline of a crescent moon that is a symbol of her being selected as a fledgling vampyre, Zoey believes that her Cherokee features, coupled with the exotic-looking tattoo, make her look wild—as if she belongs in ancient times when the world was more "barbaric."

After she's Marked and her life changes forever, Zoey is lost, confused, and scared. She first turns to her family for help, but her mother and step-loser-father turn a cold shoulder, making her feel like a freak. Zoey is desperate for help and guidance—and she finds it by going to her beloved Cherokee grand-mother, Sylvia Redbird. Sylvia becomes a very important human character in the series, representing and reinforcing Zoey's connection to her Cherokee roots—a foundation that turns out to be a surprisingly useful one in helping Zoey deal with her new life. Throughout the series, her grandmother is there when Zoey needs someone most.

On that visit to her grandmother's lavender farm, Zoey has a fated encounter with the immortal Nyx, and that encounter, too, is steeped in her Cherokee bloodline. The Goddess comes to her in a vision after Zoey falls and hits her head. In what appears to be a dream or hallucination, she hears familiar sounds on the wind (*U-no-le*). Ancient Cherokee voices chant in time with the rhythmic beat of the ceremonial drums of her ancestors, with their ghostly bodies "shimmering like heat waves lifting from a blacktop road in the summer," and Zoey finally meets the vampyre Goddess, Nyx, in the Cherokee realm of the Spirit People (*Nunne 'hi*).

Zoey carries her Cherokee heritage with her into the House of Night, taking the name "Zoey Redbird" to honor that heritage and her grandmother. ("Red-bird" means "daughter of the sun" in Cherokee, an irony considering that Zoey is marked by Nyx as one of her Children of the Night.) Later, we learn Zoey is the reincarnation of a Cherokee woman named A-ya (a Cherokee word meaning "me"), and the legend of A-ya, Kalona, and the Raven Mockers becomes a driving force behind the House of Night series and a motivating gem that sets the book apart from other vampire mythos.

Because of her heritage, Zoey is special even before the start of her second life as a fledgling vampyre, and it is her connection to the Cherokee people through her grandmother and A-ya that makes her uniquely able to face the threat of Neferet and Kalona. The world created in the House of Night series is a dark, rich tapestry of demons, evil spirits, and vampyres woven into real

Cherokee beliefs and traditions. It's a world threatened by legendary evil brought to life—and because of that evil's Cherokee origins, only a heroine with Cherokee roots can save it.

## THE CHEROKEE IN OKLAHOMA

The House of Night series is set in northeast Oklahoma, in Tulsa, and many local (and very real) hotspots are mentioned in the novels. The capital of the Cherokee Nation—one of three federally recognized Cherokee tribes—is located in Tahlequah, Oklahoma, seventy miles southeast of Tulsa, where the Cherokee Nation maintains over 66,000 acres of land. The Native American inspiration in the series comes naturally as part of the setting and resonates with authenticity.

Nine percent of the entire population of Oklahoma is of Native American descent, and a large part of that percentage is Cherokee; the Cherokee Nation is the largest Indian tribe in Oklahoma, with more than 290,000 citizens. The influence of the Cherokee culture can be seen in many ways in this part of Oklahoma, from street and park names like Tahlequah Road and Sequoyah State Park, to arts and crafts like basket-weaving, marble-making, and coloring fabric with dyes made from weeds and tree bark. Cherokee clothing styles, such as the Cherokee Ribbon Shirt and the Tear Dress, are still worn in the area.

But it's not by accident that the Cherokee have roots in Oklahoma. A tragic page in U. S. history chronicles how they were forced from their homes back East and relocated to the Midwest against their will. During the 1800s, the U.S. government designated Oklahoma as Indian Territory and rounded up all the eastern Native American tribes to relocate there, uprooting them from the only hunting grounds and lands they knew. Americans called it Indian Removal, but the Cherokee had a more fitting name—The Trail of Tears.

While some tribes agreed to the relocation, others did not. Those that refused were forced to go anyway by U.S. troops. The Cherokee Nation was one of the largest of the eastern tribes who refused to make the move. They had been peaceful allies to the United States and asked for the Supreme Court to intervene on their behalf. The high court decided in favor of the Cherokee, ruling that they could stay in their homes, but President Andrew Jackson sent his army to force the Cherokee out despite the Supreme Court's decision. Thousands of Cherokee and other Natives died in the treacherous journey across the country. It was winter and many were not prepared for such a grueling trip. It was a dark time in U.S. history.

But the Cherokee Nation survived.

Today, members of the Cherokee Nation live primarily in fourteen counties in northeastern Oklahoma. The Cherokee Nation holds significant businesses, corporations, real estate, and agricultural interests, and they have become an influential and positive force in Oklahoma. They are integrated into every aspect of daily life within the state, but they have sovereign status granted to them by treaty and law. The Cherokee have their own tax code and raise taxes to provide governmental services for their citizens, subsidized by their casino operations. They maintain health clinics throughout Oklahoma, contribute to community development programs, build roads and bridges, and construct schools and universities for their citizens. A Marshal Service employs law enforcement officers that live within the fourteen county jurisdictions. In short, the Cherokee in Oklahoma are doing everything in their power to sustain and revitalize their culture. The Cherokee language is being preserved, historic sites are being restored, and museums are being endowed. And the Cherokee's ancient history, culture, and ceremonies are being honored.

The Cherokee people are not simply a people defined by their past; they intend to be an integral part of the future, as well. As Cherokee spiritual leader Redbird Smith wrote, "The fires kept burning are merely emblematic of the greater Fire, the greater Light, the Great Spirit. I realize now as never before, it is not only for the Cherokees, but for all mankind."

With the ancient blood of a proud and enduring people running through her veins, it is no wonder that Zoey Redbird is such a courageous heroine.

## THE CHEROKEE MATRIARCHAL SOCIETY—
## THEN & NOW

With other Native American tribes to choose from, why did the authors of the House of Night series pick the Cherokee as Zoey's ancestors? One reason is that the Cherokee are a vital part of the Tulsa setting and culture, but perhaps another answer can be found in a closer examination of Cherokee society.

Women have always played and continue to play an important role in the Cherokee Nation. Traditionally, the Cherokee were farming people, and unlike other, more nomadic tribes, they lived in settled villages, usually located near water. Women harvested crops and gathered berries, nuts, and fruit to eat. They also cared for the young and the elderly, and made clothing, instruments, weapons, and tools. Men traded, made war, handled diplomacy, and hunted (though women were known to occasionally hunt buffalo alongside them and even go into battle). Both genders took part in storytelling, artwork, music, and traditional medicine, but women were the landowners. In short, women were in charge of farming, property, and family. And while men made political decisions for the tribe, women made social decisions for their clans.

In Cherokee society, there can be many clans within the larger context of a tribe. Today, the Cherokee Nation's seven clans are purely bureaucratic artifacts of ancient Cherokee culture, but even now, family lines are still determined by the mother's clan. Children automatically become members of the mother's clan at birth. (Consequently, if a non-Cherokee woman marries a Cherokee man, the children of that union would not have a clan and traditionally would not be considered Cherokee.)

In the past, each matrilineal clan was run by its own Council of Women, a group of Clan Grandmothers led by a Beloved Woman (or *Ghigua*). Ghigua were chosen on an annual basis and were picked for many reasons: for bravery in battle, or for some other noteworthy quality, such as a knowledge of healing or an ability to make fair and just decisions for the clan. This recognition was the greatest honor a Cherokee woman could receive. In addition to acting as the head of her clan's Council of Women, every Ghigua held a prestigious voting seat in the tribe's main political body, the Council of Chiefs. The Cherokee Council of Chiefs was historically comprised of the clans' male chiefs, but anyone could attend and speak at a council meeting, including women. The Chiefs listened to discussion on issues brought to the council before recommending a course of action and waiting for a consensus, which would then become their final ruling. And women had considerable influence in these debates.

If an individual broke ancient Cherokee laws, they were brought before the appropriate Clan Grandmothers for judgment. These women were strict and would show no mercy to those who had committed serious breaches of social conduct. The decisions and rulings of these Grandmothers were not questioned. They also acted as their people's advisors and guides and served as ambassadors and peace negotiators between the clans. Grandmothers of one clan would also join with the Grandmothers of other clans when important decisions needed to be made for the whole village or tribe.

Clan Grandmothers are still highly respected, obeyed, and honored today. Because of the Council of Women and the role of the *Ghigua*, respect for women in Cherokee society has been passed down through the generations. Today, Cherokee women can be Chiefs and have full votes in all councils. (The first woman to serve on the Council of Chiefs as a Chief herself was Wilma P. Mankiller, who was Principal Chief—the head of the Council— from 1985–1995.)

Ghigua no longer exist in our world—the last official Cherokee Ghigua was Nancy Ward, who died in 1822. But in the House of Night series, Kalona uses the term to refer to Sylvia Redbird in *Hunted*. And when Sylvia tells Zoey the legend of Kalona and A-ya in *Untamed*, she says it's the Ghigua Women of the Cherokee that created A-ya and trapped Kalona underground. The duties of the Ghigua in the House of Night may be a little different than in the real world, but their job was the same: to protect their clan and tribe. With Zoey Redbird coming from such a strong lineage of empowered women, it isn't a stretch to believe she can be the most powerful High Priestess the House of Night has ever seen.

## TRADITIONAL CHEROKEE RITUAL AND BELIEF

Respect for women isn't the only thing the Cherokee and the House of Night's vampyre society have in common. Cherokee spiritual beliefs contain a similar idea of the sacred. They respect nature, revere the earth and its animals, and honor their elders and ancestors. These basic tenets are reflected in Zoey, but they came from Sylvia Redbird and the teachings of her people—teachings that, while they have their origins in an ancient beliefs system, have evolved and are integrated into day-to-day life of many Cherokee today. For instance, certain numbers still play a fundamental role in Cherokee ceremonies, like the numbers four and seven, which repeatedly occur in myths, stories, and rituals. Four represents the four basic directions of east, west, north, and south. The number seven refers to the seven Cherokee clans.

## The Seven Clans of the Cherokee

The names of the seven clans of the Cherokee people represent the spiritual forces that shape and guide humanity on its journey through life, in preparation for entry into the spirit world.

*Anigilohi* (the Long Hair Clan): the human people
*Anisahoni* (the Blue Holly Clan): purification in preparation for ceremonies
*Aniwaya* (the Wolf Clan): the doorway to the world of spirits and the development of a higher social consciousness
*Anigatogewi* (the Wild Potato Clan): earth or physical matter
*Anikawi* (the Deer Clan): the spirit of life or procreation
*Anitsiskwa* (the Bird or Red-tailed Hawk Clan): the development of the human intellect
*Aniwodi* (the Paint Clan): the four directions, the structure of society, and the evolution of social organization

The number seven is also associated with purity and sacredness, a challenging state to attain. In the animal kingdom, both the owl and cougar are believed to have reached such a state, and one Cherokee creation story explains that this is because they were the only two animals able to stay awake during the seven days of the Creation. (That's why they are nocturnal animals today, according to legend. Perhaps the same is true of vampyres.) The pine, cedar, spruce, holly, and laurel had achieved this rank of sacredness because they, too, stayed awake—which is why they all play an important role in Cherokee ceremonies and medicines even today. Cedar is the most sacred of all. The wood from the tree is considered very revered, and in ancient times, it was used to carry the honored dead (Sylvia recommends cedar needles be burned while Stark travels to the Otherworld). Rivers, or "Long Man," are also sacred, and water is used for purification by the Cherokee, as Zoey mentions learning from her grandmother in *Marked*.

Sylvia taught Zoey many things about her sacred Cherokee culture and spiritual values that turn out to be very useful to Zoey when her life changes. At the end of *Marked*, Zoey relies on her knowledge of Cherokee rituals as well as the protection of Nyx to fortify her before she confronts Aphrodite. Specifically, she uses a variation on a purification ritual to summon positive energy. As Zoey says, traditional Cherokee purification rituals are usually performed with running water nearby. But when running water isn't available on school grounds for her to conduct her ritual (or at least not anywhere private), she decides to use a smudging stick instead and holds her ceremony under a massive oak tree where she had found her cat Nala. (Oaks are also revered by the Cherokee.) To magnify her prayer, Zoey conducts her ceremony before dawn, along with her grandmother who performs the ritual simultaneously at her lavender farm.

The simultaneous rituals at dawn and the words of the prayer are fiction, a product of the authors' creativity, but there is a traditional Cherokee practice that Zoey's predawn purification ritual closely reflects, called "going to water." This ritual, which is still practiced by some Cherokee today, is performed at sunrise, and involves facing east and immersing oneself in water seven times to cleanse both body and spirit.

The smudging ritual, too, is an authentic part of Cherokee beliefs. In smudging, the Cherokee do use different types of herbs or plants, including sage, cedar, and sweetgrass. Sage is believed to drive out evil spirits, negative thoughts, and feelings, and keep *Gan'n* (negative entities) away from the people, places, and things protected by the ceremony. (In a traditional sweat lodge, the floor of the lodge is strewn with sage so the Cherokee can rub it on their bodies during the sweat to protect themselves.) And the way Zoey uses sage reflects a traditional method of smudging, in which the herbs are burned in a bundled "wand" and the smoke is directed with a hand or feather over the person, place, or thing to be protected. However, the white sage and lavender Zoey uses is not a traditional combination for smudging. Instead, it reflects her own preference for lavender, perhaps because it reminds her of her grandmother.

In Zoey's ritual, she takes her cue from the circle cast at the Dark Daughters' Full Moon Ritual. The Dark Daughters' circle has a strong impact on Zoey, stirring the elements of Air, Fire, Water, Earth, and Spirit within her, but the circle is a familiar symbol to Cherokees today, as well. The Stomp Dance and other tribal ceremonies involve moving in a circle pattern. And in Cherokee history, the Native council built its fires by arranging the wood so the flames would burn in a circular pathway. In Zoey's circle, she and her friends each hold a colored candle to represent the five elements: purple for Spirit, red for Fire, green for Earth, blue for Water, and yellow for Air. The Cherokee also have spiritual associations with certain colors, but in their case the colors are associated with the seven directions they hold as sacred: North (blue), South (white), East (red), West (black), Sun (yellow), Earth (brown), and Self (green).

When Zoey starts smudging, she begins by wafting the herb smoke at the feet and works up the body, front and back. She does this for each of the four members of her circle, beginning with Damien, who is positioned on the east side of the circle, before handing the smudge stick to Stevie Rae, who smudges Zoey, as well. Then, Zoey speaks an adapted version of the Cherokee Purification Prayer that her grandmother taught her (modified to pay homage to the vampyres' Goddess), again beginning while facing the east and moving through each of the other directions in turn. The smudging ritual is traditionally performed in all four directions, too: East, West, North, and South.

Later in *Marked*, Aphrodite uses a smudge stick as well—except, as Zoey notes, she doesn't smudge with sage first to purify and skips right to burning sweetgrass, which attracts spirits both good and bad. Because she doesn't have a good understanding of herb usage, Aphrodite conducts a ritual that goes very wrong, and as evil spirits invade her ceremony, she has no idea how to stop what happens until Zoey steps in. But the practice of summoning the bad before cleansing it away is actually a traditional Cherokee practice: sweetgrass is used in combination with sage to summon bad spirits or negativity first before they are cleansed away by burning sage.

There are a few other Native American symbols and rituals of note in the series, though they aren't strictly Cherokee in origin. In *Untamed*, Sylvia rushes to help Zoey after Raven Mockers invade the House of Night campus and Kalona begins to infiltrate Zoey's dreams and Aphrodite's visions. Sylvia brings two items with her: protective pillar candles and dream catchers, described in *Untamed* as a "leather wrapped circle with lavender-colored string webbed inside, and caught within the center of the web was a smooth turquoise stone, the breathtaking blue of a summer sky. The feathers that hung in three tiers from the sides and the bottom were the pearl gray of a dove." After Sylvia advises the girls to hang the dream catchers in their windows by their beds, she tells them that dream catchers do more than attract good dreams. She says they guard against bad ones and protect the owner's sleeping soul from harm. Although protective pillar candles and dream catchers can't be directly linked to specific Cherokee legends the way they are referenced in the series, their use does accentuate aspects of Native American beliefs. Pillar candles, for instance, have an herbal aroma that many believe creates an aura of protection, and the candles themselves empower spells and rituals by the energy derived from them. And while the creation of dream catchers is attributed to the Ojibwe People, many Native American tribes (not including the Cherokee) have references to them.

In Native American culture, dreams hold great power and drift in the night, coming to those asleep. To keep the dreamer safe, tribal elders created dream catchers, a special web inside a circle with dangling ornamentation, usually beads and feathers, that hung near the places where people slept in lodges and teepees, or on baby cradleboards. Similar to what Sylvia tells the girls, when bad dreams traveled through the web, they lost their way and got entangled, only to be destroyed by the first rays of daybreak. Good dreams, though, know the way and always travel through the open center of the web, finding a path to the sleeper.

The turquoise in the center of Sylvia's dream catcher plays a role in Native American beliefs, as well. In many Native American cultures, turquoise is known as "sky stone" and is considered a sign of well-being, good health, and luck. Unlike in the House of Night series, however, where Sylvia also uses a handful of crushed turquoise to repel a Raven Mocker from Zoey's window, it has no special ability to ward off evil—though in some Native American cultures, it is believed to have protective qualities. Throughout the series, we see Zoey take the real Cherokee practices her grandmother taught her and adjust them for her needs, adapting them to the circumstances she faces in the series. The Casts do the same thing when they take real-world Cherokee traditions and adapt them to the needs of their story. They possess the same deep respect and appreciation for Cherokee beliefs they have instilled in Zoey.

## Cherokee Herb Gathering Practices

The Cherokee people have many gifts they believe come from the Creator, much as the House of Night's vampyres have gifts and affinities they believe come from Nyx. And one of the most treasured in Cherokee society is the understanding of the gathering, use, and conservation of medicinal herbs. In the traditional practice of herb gathering, the Cherokee ask the plant's permission to be gathered and sometimes leave a small gift as a token of gratitude, such as a bead or other memento. Such a practice speaks to the respect the Cherokee have for the earth and the Creator.

Cherokee believe plants were put on earth to not only heal or to purify (as in the smudging ritual), but to prevent illness, too. A word of caution, however: plants and herbs can be very valuable as medicines, but they can also be dangerous if used the wrong way. Cherokee herbalists have a great deal of experience and have extensive training, like the lessons Zoey received under the guidance of her grandmother, but novices should seek advice on how fresh-picked herbs and plants can be identified and utilized for healing and as preventive medicines.

AS ZOEY Redbird faces mythical creatures in a classic battle between good and evil in the House of Night series, she brings Cherokee traditions alive for the reader. Zoey's link to her Native American heritage adds depth and humanity to the story, as the authors bring twists of creativity to some of the most compelling and authentic Cherokee traditions. And while the series may not be reliable as a factual representation of Cherokee culture, the proud history of the Cherokee People still serves as a constant source of inspiration for the authors and makes Zoey Redbird one of the most original heroines in young adult fiction.

**JORDAN DANE** launched her back-to-back debut suspense novels in 2008 after the three books sold in auction. Ripped from the headlines, Jordan's gritty plots weave a tapestry of vivid settings, intrigue, and dark humor. *Publishers Weekly* compared her intense pacing to Lisa Jackson, Lisa Gardner, and Tami Hoag—naming her debut book, *No One Heard Her Scream*, as one of the Best Books of 2008. And Harlequin Teen is releasing two young adult novels by Dane: *In the Arms of Stone Angels* (April 2011) and *On a Dark Wing* (TBA 2012). Jordan and her husband share their Texas residence with two cats and a rescue dog named Taco. For more, visit www.JordanDane.com.

# { Freedom of Choice }

## KALONA, A-YA, AND THE RAVEN MOCKERS

*Jeri Smith-Ready*

IT'S NOT easy being the Chosen One. Just ask Buffy Summers. Ask Harry Potter. And ask Zoey Redbird, the latest in this list of "lucky" candidates picked by fate to save the world from darkness—and oh yeah, find romance, keep their friends, and maybe not flunk every class. In their spare time, of course.

You'd think the act of getting chosen would be the biggest hurdle of all. Once you know you're The One, every choice should be easy. Simply "do the right thing," and the rest will follow. After all, you were chosen for a reason, so you must be destined to succeed, right?

Alas, destiny isn't a straight, well-paved road. Sometimes it's not even a rocky, overgrown bike path. All the signs point in different directions, and half of them aren't even in English (they might be in another language—or worse, *poetry*).

The adults or divine beings—you know, the ones who have let things get so messed up in the first place—hand you a huge assignment: go forth, fight evil, here are some superpowers. Good luck!

*Ah, hell*, as Zoey would say. Now what?

Good question. How can a mere fledgling make the right choices when even immortals can't get it right?

Look at Kalona—he was Nyx's pledged Warrior, a bond that demands and rewards the utmost loyalty and devotion. Yet he squandered his Goddess' loving trust. After his banishment, rather than trying to get back into Nyx's good graces, he spent centuries piling up one offense after another. The half-human Raven Mockers he sired brought even more misery into the world, misery they can't entirely blame on their evil heritage. Of all these mythical beings, A-ya alone, a human creation, lacks the ability to make a choice.

Every human and immortal character, every player in the battle for the soul of the world, has the power to choose the path of darkness or light, no matter how far down one path they've already walked.

Or flown, as the case may be . . .

## "DARK SPIRITS OF THE WORST TYPE": THE RAVEN MOCKERS

In the House of Night series, we first meet the Raven Mockers at the beginning of *Untamed*, when Zoey hears a raven's call as she feels a sudden chill and a flapping in the air around her, along with the sense that someone—or some*thing*—is watching. Aphrodite later has a vision of one of these creatures killing Zoey by slicing her throat. Sylvia Redbird, Zoey's grandmother, describes them as "ravens, with the eyes and limbs of man" and "mischief makers—dark spirits that take pleasure from annoying the living and tormenting those at the cusp of death."

Grandma Redbird's description of the Raven Mockers' activities—if not their appearance—is taken directly from the legends of her people. In Cherokee mythology, the Raven Mockers, or *Kâ'lanû Ahkyeli'skî* (Anglicized as *Kalona Ayeliski*), are evil spirits of either gender who rob dying people of their lives. Usually they appear to the old and sick, who may report seeing fiery figures flying, arms outstretched and calling like ravens as they descend. They may also see pale, shriveled figures—like very old men and women—huddled at their bedside. This aged appearance is supposed to reflect the many lives they have stolen.

Once the Raven Mockers have arrived, they torment the weak person to hasten his or her death. Then they consume the heart of the deceased. By doing so, they add days or years to their own lives at the expense of their victims (i.e., the extra time that the victim would have lived has been added to the life of the Raven Mocker).

Though usually invisible to everyone but the sick and dying, the Raven Mockers can be seen by medicine men, who are often employed to guard the stricken ones until they have either died in peace or recovered. Any Raven Mocker who dares to appear in the presence of a medicine man is likely to die within seven days.

## What a Difference a Week Makes

The seven-day period is a common one in many mythologies and stories.

- In Genesis, God is said to have created the world in six days, using the seventh to rest (hence the creation of the Sabbath).

- In Cherokee creation mythology, the animals were asked to stay awake for seven nights. All but the owl and the cougar fell asleep, so these two animals were gifted with night vision.

- Also in Cherokee creation mythology, the first woman gave birth to a new person every seven days until the earth became overpopulated, at which point the birthrate was cut back to once per year.

- In *Burned*, Zoey can only dwell in the Otherworld for seven days before her soul completely dissipates and the earth is in big trouble.

According to James Moody's *History, Myths, and Sacred Formulas of the Cherokees* (a great resource on Cherokee myths!), the Raven Mockers are only one type of Cherokee witch, but they are the most terrible. Even other witches fear and hate them, and when a Raven Mocker dies, the witches will take revenge by digging up the body and abusing it. As Zoey's grandmother is quick to point out, Cherokee witches are evil—nothing like the modern-day, earth-embracing followers of Wicca.

## On the Wings of Night

One Cherokee term for witch, *tskĭlĭ'*, can be Anglicized as *Tsi Sgili*—the name Neferet loves to call herself. *Tskĭlĭ'* is also the word for the bird species known as the great-horned owl. Among Cherokees, owls are thought to be witches in disguise. Another term for witch is *sûnnâ'yĭedâ'hĭ*, or "night goer," since they are thought to appear mostly after dark. Hmm, just like vampires . . .

So where do the Raven Mockers come from? Who or what created them? Cherokee myth gives us no hint. They just are. They always have been. Good and evil exist, pure and simple, and Raven Mockers are evil. Period.

That's where the Casts come in.

## "BEAUTIFUL BEYOND COMPARE":
## KALONA THE BETRAYER

The House of Night series provides a compelling origin story for the Raven Mockers, a story reminiscent of the ultimate Christian villain himself.

As imagined by P.C. and Kristin Cast, Kalona is an immortal being who was originally a Warrior sworn to the Goddess Nyx. His oath bound him to protect her from Darkness, but when he turned away from her, jealous of her consort Erebus, she banished him from the Otherworld forever.

Kalona's fall from the Otherworld bears several parallels to the legends of Lucifer, especially as portrayed in John Milton's 1667 epic poem, *Paradise Lost*. Like Kalona, Lucifer was once the most glorious and beautiful of angels, a being of light. "Lucifer," in fact, means "Light Giver," and he is sometimes referred to as Morningstar or "son of the morning" (Isaiah 14). Like Kalona, Lucifer's beautiful white wings turned black when he fell (though in *Paradise*

*Lost* he loses his feathers entirely and gets big ugly bat wings, as his outward appearance starts to reflect his inward evil).

## Not-So-Dark Secrets about Lucifer

Fun fact: The planet Venus—aka, the "morning star" when it appears before sunrise, outshining all the stars in the heavens—was once known as Lucifer.

Funner fact: The chemical that makes fireflies' butts light up is called "luciferin."

And like Kalona, Lucifer became jealous when someone else took his place as most favored of his beloved—just substitute the eternal Son in heaven (and eventually humans on earth) for Erebus and God the Father for Nyx. Though Lucifer and Kalona held exalted roles, it wasn't enough. Both immortals' pride got the better of them, causing their rebellion and expulsion from their beautiful homes.

In *Untamed*, both Zoey's grandmother and Sister Mary Angela compare Kalona to the Nephilim, the legendary angels who fell from heaven and are said to have mated with mortal women on earth. Grandma Redbird says that Goliath (of David and Goliath fame) is sometimes said to have been one of the Nephilim, who were all of superhuman size and strength.

But while Lucifer (or Satan, as he is called after the Fall) rejected the notion of love and embraced his sin of pride—uttering the infamous line, "Better to reign in Hell than serve in Heaven"—Kalona continues to delude himself that he did it all for love. His is a perverted conception of love, however, requiring absolute control and obedience. In his scenes with Zoey, he professes his utmost devotion to her—until she questions or rejects him, and then he inevitably launches into an immortal-sized sulkfest.

In *Burned*, the Raven Mocker Rephaim tells Stevie Rae that he and his brothers were born from Kalona's rage and bitterness at being tossed from the Otherworld. This is metaphorically true, though a bit of a stretch. After all, the Raven Mockers didn't just pop out of Kalona's head. For them to exist, he had to act—and act badly.

By connecting Kalona to the Raven Mockers, the House of Night series compellingly fits this fictional immortal being into existing Cherokee mythology. After Nyx's rejection, Kalona dwelled on earth along with other fallen angels, according to Grandma Redbird. He appeared to the Cherokee people, who worshipped him in gratitude for their healthy crops and fertile women.

Of course, mere praise wasn't enough for him. Kalona's unspent lust (or what his supernatural powers of rationalization would call his unrequited longing for Nyx) drove him to sleep with the women of the tribe. The Cherokee grew disillusioned and spurned him, but rather than leaving, Kalona became rapacious and domineering, feeding his insatiable appetite for power and sex. Those he raped gave birth to the Raven Mockers.

Kalona's second downfall is told through the story of another figure created for the House of Night—A-ya. Since mere human warriors couldn't stop Kalona, "a creature of myth and magic," the Wise Women got together to figure out how to defeat him. As an immortal being, Kalona obviously couldn't be killed. But perhaps he could be trapped by his two weaknesses—his hunger for women and his vulnerability to the earth. So the Wise Women sculpted from clay a beautiful, irresistible maiden, A-ya, and breathed life into her. (A-ya means "me" in the Cherokee language, perhaps indicating that this maiden was to represent all women or even all humanity.)

Interestingly, this process is much like that described in tales of the *golem* in Jewish tradition. In Hebrew, golem stands for "unformed substance" or "shapeless mass." To create a golem, one would sculpt a man-shaped figure out of clay and then bring it to life with some form of the word "God," since God is the creator of all life. This could involve chanting the secret name of God, or writing the name of God on a piece of parchment and inserting it into the golem's mouth.

The most fascinating animation method involved carving the letters *aleph*, *mem*, and *tav* into the golem's forehead. Together these three letters spell *emet*, or "truth." When you were done with your golem, you could "kill" it by erasing the letter *aleph*, leaving the word *met*, or "death." While "alive," the creature could follow simple instructions, but it couldn't think for itself and it had no will, like a robot made of dirt.

This lack of will is crucial, because A-ya was literally made to love Kalona. She had no choice, no thoughts, and therefore no fear of him, unlike the mortal women. A-ya lured Kalona into an underground cave, where, as a winged creature of the air, he would be weakest. Deep within the earth, A-ya opened herself to Kalona willingly. As he penetrated her, she transformed back to earth, and he became trapped in her embrace forever.

With the loss of their father, the Raven Mockers became insubstantial creatures of pure spirit, no longer able to hurt the young and healthy. They sang a new song, swearing that one day Kalona would rise again and exact revenge. He would once again dominate men and violate women—and they would like it. In Aphrodite's vision, Grandma Redbird held a paper with a poem describing his return:

> *Kalona's song sounds sweet*
> *As we slaughter with cold heat.*

In *Untamed*, Kalona rises from the earth, bidden by Neferet and released by the shedding of Stevie Rae's blood ("When earth's power bleeds sacred red"). He fixates on Zoey, whom he believes to be the reincarnation of A-ya.

Through dreams, visions, and the power of her own intuition, Zoey slowly accepts that she shares part of this ancient maiden's soul. But unlike A-ya, she can think for herself. She can deny the feelings within her that draw her so strongly to Kalona.

It isn't easy by a long shot. Most other fledglings and even adult vampyres can't resist his pull. He's powerful and smooth-talking and ZOMG-hot. He claims to be Erebus, the consort of the very Goddess whom the fledglings and vampyres adore. He tells them everything they want to hear, how they should rule the world and bring back "the old ways, where once vampyres and their Warriors strode the earth, proud and strong, instead of hiding in clusters in schools…Vampyres are Nyx's children, and the Goddess never meant for you to cower in darkness." After two alleged human-on-vampyre murders at the Tulsa House of Night, his audience is primed for his leadership and liberation. According to one of Aphrodite's visions, Zoey herself will reign with Kalona if she gives in to him.

For Zoey, the allure of Kalona is ten times greater than it is for anyone else, because the part of her soul that she shares with A-ya was made to love him. She recognizes his great beauty and the power of his temptation, but that's not what attracts her most—she is drawn to him by pity and compassion, and holds out hope that he can return to Nyx's ways.

But as Nyx says in the beginning of the series when she appears to Zoey in a vision and fills in her Mark, this is "a world where good and evil are struggling to find balance" (*Marked*). We see this struggle for cosmic balance enacted inside Zoey, as well—while part of her was made to love Kalona, part of her was also made to destroy him. When she sees him kill Heath in cold blood, she realizes that despite Kalona's occasional remorse, he has chosen evil again and again, and always will.

## A PRICE PAID IN PAIN: REPHAIM'S REDEMPTION

Meanwhile, Kalona's firstborn and favorite son, Rephaim, becomes part of another drama of choices, with an entirely different outcome from his father's. Mortally wounded in *Hunted*'s climactic battle, Rephaim is saved at the beginning of *Tempted* by Stevie Rae, herself no stranger to darkness. Her recent death, un-death, and subsequent bloodthirsty rampage allow her to have sympathy for the fallen half-mortal spirit. She remembers that despite the intentions of Neferet, who brought her back from the dead, she was able to choose good and control her violent urges. Stevie Rae may therefore be the only person capable of seeing Rephaim's humanity, and it is this humanity that she pledges herself to in *Burned*, as part of a bargain with the Black Bull in exchange for Rephaim's life.

In *Tempted*, Rephaim saves Stevie Rae's life to pay her back for saving his, to rid himself of that debt. But in *Burned*, Rephaim saves her for another reason—because he loves her (though he wouldn't call it that). When Darkness in the form of the White Bull is torturing her, Rephaim is able to heal himself, fly to her, and break through the circle she's cast, all because he is connected to Darkness. Just as Stevie Rae could sympathize with him because she has touched Darkness in her past, he is only able to save her from Darkness *because* of Darkness itself.

But it's more than that. He only convinces Darkness to let her go by finding the humanity inside himself, the part his human mother bestowed, the part that lets him say, "I'm here because she's here, and she belongs to me."

Saving her life the first time cost him nothing, but this time he must offer himself to Darkness in her place. He suffers even more than Stevie Rae has, for his immortal blood is more irresistible than hers, and because he uses Darkness to gain enough power to heal and break the circle, so he must pay his own debt as well as hers. It's only Stevie Rae's bargain with the Black Bull (Light) that saves him. They belong to each other.

## World's Biggest Losers

The word *Rephaim* refers to an ancient biblical people possibly related to the Nephilim (or fallen angels—remember them?). The Rephaim, also called the Rephaites, were thought to have been a race of giants. King Og of Bashan, the last of the Rephaim, is described in Deuteronomy as having a nine-cubit (fourteen-foot-long) bed. (Interestingly, the term for dead people or departed spirits may be rooted in a similar Hebrew word, *repaim*.) The Bible doesn't mention that these people committed any major crimes other than living in the Promised Land, but that was enough to warrant wiping them out.

## A DOUBLE-EDGED SWORD

So why would P.C. and Kristin modify the Raven Mocker myth, creating such a fantastic origin story in the form of Kalona?

Two words: Free. Will. Throughout the House of Night series, Zoey is faced with choices. She doesn't always make the "right" one. Her actions sometimes even hurt herself and others (Loren Blake, anyone?). But as is often repeated, the Goddess Nyx's greatest gift to her children is free will. Love and goodness are meaningless without the ability to choose their opposites.

Like Lucifer, Kalona had a choice between light and darkness, and he freely chose darkness, not only when he fell from the Otherworld, but again and again on earth. By making Kalona's rage and pride the source of the Raven

Mockers, the Casts give the Raven Mockers a thematic reason for existing, rather than being mindless "evil spirits" who came from nowhere. And as we see with Rephaim, even these creatures born of rape and blood have the capacity for love when shown compassion and understanding. They are, after all, born of human women, and have humanity in them.

Despite Zoey's status as A-ya reincarnated and Chosen of Nyx, she can still choose darkness. Darkness can take the form of not only active evil, but also inaction—choosing her own happiness and peace at the expense of the world. Many times she wishes to be normal and not carry the burden given to her. The fact that Zoey has more than one possible path is illustrated explicitly in Aphrodite's visions—they are never what *will* be, but what *might* be—and more than once, Aprhodite has competing, contradictory visions. The future is always in flux.

Zoey is highly imperfect, as are those who surround her—friends, boy-friends, enemies, and protectors alike. Characters who are initially drawn to darkness—such as Stark, Aphrodite, and Rephaim—make hard choices to be heroic when it counts, even if it means losing who they think they are, or even losing their lives. As Stevie Rae returns from the dead, she has a long, difficult journey back to Light. Kalona himself has the potential to turn away from pride and toward love, but by the end of *Burned*, he has made his choice of Darkness forever clear.

It could be argued that the ability of these characters to make mistakes, to fall—to *fail*—is part of what makes the series so appealing. As in life, there are no guarantees, and Zoey does her best to muddle through and do the right thing, despite exhaustion/injury/near-death, confusion, and major boyfriend drama. It's all Nyx asks of anyone who serves Her.

Because without choice—without freedom—love is hollow. You could win someone over by giving them a love potion, and at first you'd be happy just to have their affections. But soon, it would feel empty. You'd know that they had no choice, and that their feelings weren't earned or real.

Just as no human in their right mind should be satisfied with a love potion-derived relationship, no true deity should want to force obedience and devotion. God himself puts it best in *Paradise Lost*, when discussing the rebel angels:

*Freely they stood who stood, and fell who fell.*
*Not free, what proof could they have given sincere*
*Of true allegiance, constant faith or love,*
*Where only what they needs must do, appeared,*
*Not what they would?*

There is no destiny but what we choose, and Nyx wouldn't have it any other way.

JERI SMITH-READY is the author of the teen paranormal novels *Shade* and *Shift*, as well as the award-winning WVMP Radio adult vampire series, which includes *Wicked Game*, *Bad to the Bone*, and *Bring on the Night*. She lives in Maryland with her husband, two cats, and the world's goofiest greyhound. Visit her on Facebook or Twitter, or at www.jerismithready.com.

# { The Otherworld Is Greek to Me }

*Trinity Faegen*

FROM CHARACTER names to story elements, P.C. and Kristin Casts' House of Night series is a treasure trove of allusions to Greek mythology. Nyx's origins are in Greek myth—she appears in Hesiod's *Theogony*, Homer's *Illiad*, and other ancient Greek texts. Aphrodite takes her name from the Greek goddess. But the references to Greek myth that fascinate me most are those related to Nyx's Otherworld. The Casts have taken the ancient Greek's Underworld and added their own imaginative twist, creating a colorful, intriguing new answer to the eternal question, "Where do we go after we die?" Just like the Underworld in Greek mythology, selective visits to the Otherworld by the living are allowed. Also just like the Underworld, some visitors can never leave. And while the two aren't identical, there are enough similarities that it's interesting to compare and contrast.

The uncertainty of the afterlife is universal, a timeless question without an answer because all the experts are gone. With the field wide open for conjecture, there are countless myths and stories about life after death. Ancient civilizations across the globe had their own (often eerily similar) explanations for what happens after death, but thanks to rock-star writers like Hesiod and Homer, Greek myths remain the gold standard.

## Afterlife of the Ancients

In ancient times, Mesopotamians believed the dead dwelled in the Great Below, the Land of No Return, ruled by Ereshkigal. According to Alice K. Turner in *The History of Hell*, mortals lived on Earth, but patches of the other world adjoined this one. Similar to Greek myth, there are descent stories of mortals and other gods who visited the Great Below, some of whom returned to the living and some of whom didn't.

In ancient Egypt, the afterlife was complicated, and the journey to Sekhet Hetepet, ruled by benign Osiris, was perilous. There were gates, portals, and the Hall of Justice, after which, if the dead made the cut and their heart wasn't eaten by the monster Ammit, there were further dangers that could only be overcome by following instructions in the Book of the Dead. Unlike in Greek mythology, no one traveled to the other side unless they were dead, but the Otherworld of the Egyptians was so complicated, it's easy to see why. Nobody but a dead guy would go through crocodiles, snakes, giant beetles, and the risk of having their heart eaten by a monster.

Back in the day, ancient Greeks didn't think of the Underworld as a bad place. It was simply where people went after they died. But it was still dangerous. Very few living mortals visited the Underworld, but those who did were considered heroic. Who but a hero would attempt to visit the land of the dead?

One of the most famous of these visits is in Homer's *Odyssey*, the story of King Odysseus' ten-year journey home. After fighting the Trojans for ten years, he's really ready to return to his kingdom and be reunited with his loyal wife, but things don't go as planned and he faces one obstacle after another. Circe, a witch he encounters along the way, tells him he should seek the advice of a wise mortal, but since the guy she's referring to is dead, Odysseus will have to visit the Underworld to find him. He and his crew set sail and travel to the cave at Taenarum, in Greece, a portal to the Underworld. There, Odysseus sacrifices a young ram and a black ewe to the god of the Underworld, Hades. As the beasts' blood flows into a trench, Odysseus calls on the spirits to rise and meet him at the entrance to the cave. The wise mortal gives him the advice he was seeking, and he speaks to several other helpful spirits, too, before the Queen of the Underworld, Persephone, sends some not-so-savory spirits to the cave and Odysseus books a hasty retreat.

Our first glimpse of Nyx's Otherworld is early in the first book, *Marked*, when Zoey freaks out after she's been Marked as a fledgling vampyre and goes to her Grandma Redbird for help. Running from the spirits of her Cherokee ancestors because she's certain death is closing in, she trips and hits her head, knocking herself unconscious. Her blood trickles into a crevice in the ground and a woman's voice calls to her. Thinking it's Grandma Redbird, she throws her spirit into the crevasse and finds herself in a cave with a small brook, where her blood mingles with the clear water. Unlike Odysseus, Zoey doesn't purposely visit the cave; she has no idea this is part of the Otherworld, and while, yes, she was in search of counsel from her wise grandmother, it was never her intent to ask advice of someone in the spirit world. But there is a parallel between the cave at Taenarum and the cave where Zoey first meets Nyx. They are both portals to the other side, the land of gods, goddesses, and the shades of the dead. And they are both accessed by blood. Caves play a large part in Underworld myths, no doubt because ancient Greeks saw them as openings to what lies below.

To the Greeks, the concept of the Underworld was very literal—a world under the ground. When people died, their spirits were escorted down a long, winding path into the Earth until they came to the river Acheron and paid the ferryman, Charon, to take them across to the Underworld. Homer describes the descent in the *Odyssey*:

> down the dank moldering paths and past the Ocean's streams they went
> and past the White Rock and the Sun's Western Gates and past
> the Land of Dreams, and soon they reached the fields of asphodel
> where the dead, the burnt-out wraiths of mortals make their home . . .

Nyx's Otherworld is more esoteric, not a physical place, but within another realm. To visit the Otherworld, a mortal can't simply find a portal and begin the descent into the Earth, as they could in Greek mythology. Entrance to Nyx's Otherworld requires separation of the spirit from the body. Also, Grandma Redbird, in *Untamed*, uses the word "fall" to describe Kalona being cast out of the Otherworld, which implies that if the Otherworld is located anywhere, it's up, not down.

What else do we know of the Greek Underworld? It was a vast place, sectioned into three different areas that segregated its inhabitants. The Asphodel Meadows were for ordinary souls who were neither super good, nor über bad, Tartarus was reserved for those who deserved punishment, and Elysium welcomed the heroes and the virtuous. Elysium is depicted as a bright, blissful, verdant place of never-ending day. As described in Homer's *Odyssey*, "There indeed men live unlaborious days. Snow and tempest and thunderstorms never enter there, but for men's refreshment Okeanos sends out continually the high-singing breezes of the west." Within Elysium, the Elysian Fields were home to the virtuous, while the Islands of the Blessed were the afterlife realm of heroes. According to Hesiod's *Works and Days*, "They live untouched by sorrow in the Islands of the Blessed along the shore of deep swirling Okeanos, happy heroes for whom the grain-giving earth bears honey-sweet fruit flourishing thrice a year." Elysium, then, is Paradise, perhaps on par with what modern Christians and Muslims think of as Heaven.

Contrast this with what we learn of Nyx's Otherworld. Following Zoey's encounter with Nyx in the cave in *Marked*, we don't see anything more of the Otherworld until the end of *Tempted*. After Zoey witnesses Heath's murder at the hands of Kalona and attempts to strike back, her soul shatters, she falls into a coma, and her spirit awakens in the Otherworld. Like Elysium, Nyx's Otherworld—at least, what we've seen of it by the end of the seventh book—is a place of breathtaking beauty, a tranquil, pastoral Eden. Zoey is alive when she visits the other side, just like Greek heroes of old, but her journey is different. To begin with, she didn't travel there on purpose. But the key difference is that, while Zoey's spirit visits the Otherworld, her physical body does not. In all Greek myths, heroes who travel to the Underworld do so as flesh and blood mortals. The danger they face is death: traveling to the Underworld means they risk getting stuck there for good.

We learn in the next book, *Burned*, that the danger Zoey faces is also death if her spirit is away from her body for too long. But, far worse, if she can't pull the pieces of her soul together, she'll become a Caoinic Shi', one who's neither dead nor alive, doomed to restlessness for eternity. (Caoinic Shi' is not from Greek mythology, but according to P.C., is based on Gaelic words that roughly translate to "fairylike" or "ghostly.")

When Zoey awakens in the Otherworld, she has no clue where she is, and at first, she doesn't care. She's at peace, even euphoric, with no memory of what happened, and walks through a beautiful meadow, then into a grove of rowan and hawthorn. To enter Elysium, souls had to cross the river Lethe, known as the river of forgetfulness. They were made to drink the water and forget their mortal life. Zoey doesn't drink anything, but like those Greek souls, she doesn't remember who she is, or how she came to be there. Initially, her presence in the Otherworld seems like a good thing—she's happy and safely beyond Neferet and Kalona's reach. But because she's not dead, her spirit can't remain at peace for eternity. As soon as she sees Heath, she realizes this is the Otherworld and that he is there because he's dead, which she believes is her fault. Her euphoria disappears, her memory returns, and she's heartbroken all over again. The return of her memory also brings out the wraithlike figures that represent the shattered pieces of her soul, and her recognition of them is Heath's—and our—first clue that Zoey has a serious problem.

Back in the real world, James Stark is attempting to cross the boundary between this side and the other to save her. Echoing the myth of the cave at Taenarum, where Odysseus let the blood of a ram and a ewe trickle into the Underworld, Stark's blood drips into narrow trenches that disappear into the Earth, putting the Otherworld on notice that a living mortal wishes to visit. As soon as his spirit leaves his body, he faces his first obstacle: the Black Bull. Sure, the Black Bull is kind and good, Light embodied, but in a show of ultimate tough love, the bull forces Stark to prove his determination.

There are some fascinating parallels between Heracles, the greatest hero of Greek myth—or Hercules, as he was known in Roman mythology—and Stark. Heracles was the son of Zeus and a mortal woman, and Zeus' wife, Hera, was insanely jealous of her husband's lovers and their offspring. She caused trouble for the boy from the moment of his birth. Heracles managed to overcome Hera's nasty plots against him until she made him temporarily mad, and in his delusion, he killed his wife and children. When he was himself again, he was horrified by what he'd done and sought atonement. He was given twelve labors to complete, most of them completely impossible, yet he managed to accomplish each one. The last of Heracles' twelve labors was to kidnap the three-headed beast Cerberus from the Underworld. Before he descended, he took part in the Eleusinian Mysteries, an initiation rite celebrated in Ancient Greece that was believed to unite the worshipper with the gods and assure them passage to the Elysian Fields when they died. No one knows for sure what was done during the Eleusinian Mysteries, because initiates were sworn to secrecy and, incredibly, no one ever told, but what is known is that visions were involved. When Heracles was done with his initiation, he began his journey to the Underworld and was able to capture Cerebrus, completing his twelve labors.

Stark's journey follows a similar path. From the time Stark proved himself to be a prodigy archer, Neferet caused him grief, manipulating circumstances so that he would ultimately wind up at the Tulsa House of Night. After causing his untimely death, Neferet brings Stark back as a red fledgling, then commands him to use his gift of always hitting his target to shoot an arrow through Stevie Ray's heart, which results in the resurrection of Kalona. Still held in the grip of darkness, Stark doesn't want penitence. Not until he chooses Light and pledges himself Zoey's Warrior does he feel remorse. Later, when Heath is murdered and Zoey is seemingly lost to the Otherworld, Stark can't blame the hold of darkness for his failure to protect Zoey, but instead has to face the reality that his jealousy and pride left her at risk. Like Heracles, he was temporarily driven mad by a higher power and now wants atonement, and just like Heracles, his task seems impossible. When Stark confronts a vision of himself, his dark side, he must conquer it before he can continue on his quest. Like Heracles becoming an initiate of the Eleusinian Mysteries to make himself ready for and worthy of entrance to the Underworld, Stark has to become a Shaman before he can be Zoey's Guardian and gain entrance to the Otherworld.

Once Stark finally arrives, he finds Heath and Zoey within the sacred grove, a place where darkness can't enter, a safe haven where the spirit can rest. The concept of a sacred grove isn't tied to the Underworld in Greek myth, but to the reality of the living. In varying cultures, certain areas of land were set apart as the domain of gods or kings, or for other holy purposes. In Ancient Greece, there were several sacred groves, including a grove of oak trees close to Olympus that was considered sacred to Zeus.

## Will Heath Return?

When Heath says good-bye to Zoey in the Otherworld, he tells her he'll find her again, in his next life. According to the Elysium myth, an ordinary human, one who is virtuous but not heroic, could join the realm of heroes in the Islands of the Blessed if he could return to Elysium three times. And if he lived three lives worthy of returning to Elysium, he'd remain there for eternity. Reincarnation was definitely part of Greek mythology, and it seems to be part of the House of Night's as well. Heath will live again, another life, just as the ancients did. (I'd be okay with the Casts carrying on the series for a few more of Heath's lifetimes!)

Heath isn't happy to hear what Stark has to say, but he understands what he has to do to save the girl he's loved his whole life. After Heath departs, Stark begins what may be the most difficult part of his task, which is convincing Zoey to pull the pieces of her soul together so they can return to the land of the living. He realizes a crucial element in his quest to save Zoey is confronting Kalona. Heracles, after his descent to the Underworld, asked the god Hades for permission to take Cerberus. Hades agreed, on the condition that Heracles subdue Cerebus without any weapons. Stark faces Kalona with no weapon except honor and his determination to protect and champion his High Priestess. Heracles overpowers the hound of Hell through brute force, but Stark is no match for Kalona, and he dies. Why the difference, when so much of their quests parallel one another? I see Stark's sacrifice of his life for Zoey's as his atonement, not only for failing to protect her, but for all the wrongs he's done since becoming a red fledgling. Before he calls out Kalona, he tells Zoey his intent and she panics. "But you can't! You can't beat Kalona!" she tells him, and he replies, "You're probably right, Z. I can't. But *you can*" (*Burned*). He knows if Kalona kills him, Zoey will pull the pieces of her soul together and do what she must to defeat Kalona and Neferet. For Zoey, for humanity, for his honor, he challenges Kalona, knowing he's bound to die. He is truly a Guardian Shaman.

Heracles didn't die in the Underworld, but later in life he was accidentally almost killed by his second wife, who didn't realize the love potion she spread across his cloak was actually poison. Because he completed all of his appointed labors, then went on to perform even greater heroic deeds, Heracles was saved from death and made an immortal god, instead of dying like other mortals and packing it in for the Underworld. After Stark dies in the deep pit carved by Kalona's wings, Zoey demands that Kalona give him life again, and Nyx backs her up because Stark has fulfilled his quest so nobly and earned the right to live. Kalona gives Stark a part of his immortality, which brings him back from death, and to heal, Stark drinks from Zoey, forging a bond that will last eternally. Stark doesn't become a god, as Heracles did, but his experience has changed him into something he never dreamed he could be—Guardian, bonded by blood and oath to a High Priestess. I tend to think Stark appreciates this more than he would have appreciated becoming a god.

The similarities between the Underworld of Greek myth and Nyx's Otherworld are intriguing, but all we've seen thus far is something that resembles Elysium, the beautiful, serene realm of the virtuous and heroic. For now, only the Casts know if there are other, less pleasant areas on the other side. We do get a small hint from Nyx herself in *Burned*, when she reveals her Otherworld to Aphrodite in a vision. Aphrodite sees the spirits of people dancing and laughing, and asks if this is where we go after we die. Nyx replies, "Sometimes." Alarmed, Aphrodite asks what she means, if people can only go there if they're good, and Nyx says, "I am your Goddess, daughter, not your judge. Good is a multifaceted ideal." Moments later, after Aphrodite has seen what will happen if Zoey dies and says they can't let that happen, Nyx replies, "Then Heath must move on from my realm of the Otherworld." Her realm? Does this mean there are other realms of the Otherworld that are not hers? Within the Underworld, Hades is god of all, but each of the separate realms are ruled by lesser gods. We don't yet know if the Otherworld has other realms or other gods, and we may never find out. Either way, I can't wait to see what P.C. and Kristin have in store for us as the House of Night series continues.

Since she was a teen, **TRINITY FAEGEN** has been fascinated by the afterlife, probably because she read *Paradise Lost* while she was on pain meds after getting her wisdom teeth removed. She found an outlet for her curiosity about Hell by researching what other people imagined, then making up her own mythology in *The Mephisto Covenant*, a young adult novel to be released by Egmont USA in Fall 2011. Trinity lives in the outback of west Texas with her husband and a mean cat.

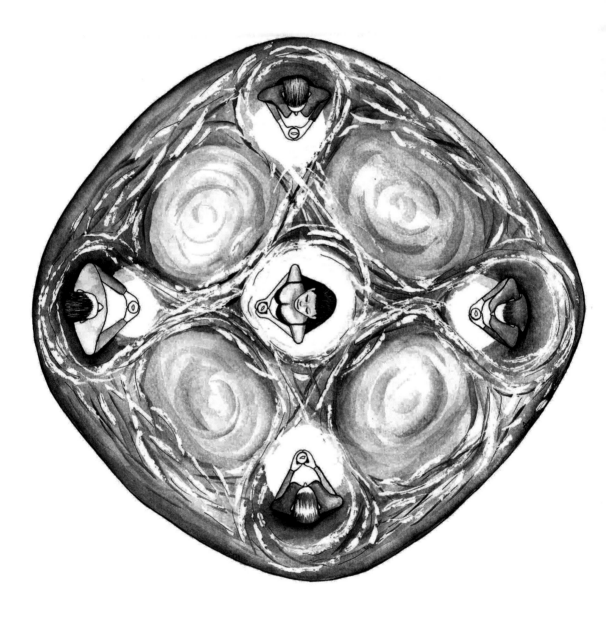

# { The Elements of Life }

# Bryan Lankford

GOOD EVENING! It's good to see this many humans who are interested in vampyre culture. As it has been many years since I've spoken to a group this large who were not vampyres, I beg your indulgence if I misspeak somewhere along the line. Tonight we are going to be discussing rituals and the elements as they are used in vampyre worship.

Many of you have read about vampyre rituals in Zoey's chronicles, but it may surprise you to know that our form of worship is not confined exclusively to the vampyre community. There are in fact many human groups who think and worship in a very similar fashion to vampyres. Human groups such as Wiccans, Pagans, Shamans, and witches all over the earth live and worship in a manner similar to us. They do not all worship our Goddess Nyx, nor do they use blood in ritual, but they do honor one, some, or all of the different variations of the Goddess and God in the diverse pantheons of deities throughout the history of mankind. These human groups also honor the elements of creation and worship in Circles as we do.

Ah . . . I've sparked an interest; you didn't realize that some humans worshipped as vampyres do. Well, the ancient practices never truly die: they just shift, form, and evolve as they travel through the corridors of time. However, as I see your curiosity about the human practices, I'll also share with you Wiccan traditions as we discuss vampyre practices, because they do overlap a great deal.

Now the first thing you're going to have to do if you're going to see the world as a vampyre or as a Wiccan is to grasp how both groups think. This may be difficult for many of you, because vampyres and Wiccans live in a very different world from the one most of you inhabit. Oh wait; I'm sensing a disturbance in the force. (What, you thought that Erik was the only vampyre who likes the Star Wars movies?) There is that explosion of protest again. I'm guessing that you're wondering how we could live in different worlds when we all inhabit the same planet? Well, in the world you inhabit do people choose their worship times by the phase of the moon and revere the changing seasons as sacred times of the year? Do you see your world as flowing with divine energy that can be gathered, focused, and directed to perform magic? In vampyre and Wiccan worlds they do, although, being human, Wiccans lack many of the more dramatic sensory elements, like lights and smells, that are present in vampyre magic. However, I have heard Wiccans have the feelings associated with magic and it is nonetheless effective to guide them, and heal the mind, body, or soul.

The point is that although we share the same planet, the worlds we inhabit, which are shaped and colored by our perceptions, are very different. If you're going to understand how vampyres and Wiccans—

Ugh. Saying vampyre and Wiccan is already becoming tedious, and I do so dislike tedious things. Therefore, from this point forward I'm just going to say "children of the earth" when I'm referring to both groups.

Where was I? Ah, yes—if you're going to understand how the children of the earth think, then the first thing you have to do is quit taking everything so literally. The language used by the children of the earth, especially when speaking about religious topics, tends to be both symbolic and metaphoric rather than concrete and literal. For those of you who need a refresher: a symbol is something that is used to stand in the place of an idea or concept. For example, an eagle might be used to represent liberty or a lion might represent courage. A baby could be used to show innocence, or an owl wisdom, and the American flag stands for all the values of being American. A metaphor, however, is a comparison between two very different things where the comparison is stated as if one were the other. For example, if you were to come stomping down the stairs in your PJs, eyes half closed and disheveled from sleep, proceed to growl at your sister to get out of your chair, and then snatch up the cereal box and start to shake it into a bowl as if she were personally responsible for that embarrassing encounter with that really cute new student when you were trying to act cool in the chemistry lab but forgot that you still had your lab goggles still plastered to your forehead and . . . oh, sorry, I digress. I spend way too much time around teens. Well anyway, if your father peered across the table and asked, "Why are you such a bear this morning?" he would be using a metaphor. There would be no need to shave a suddenly hairy face or to trim your claws. You would not actually be a bear, you would just be playing one at breakfast.

The children of the earth tend to see their religious practices in terms of symbols and metaphors that instruct people in life lessons. When we ask an element to join us in ritual we are, therefore, not asking a giant mound of intelligent dirt to appear and start a conversation. What we are asking is that the symbolic energy of that element fill us. To do that we identify the manifestations of that element in the outer world—say, the smell of fresh-mowed grass, for earth—and use that imagery to find the power of that element within ourselves. If done correctly you will feel the power, emotions, and energy of that element surround you, well within you, and flow to your extremities, filling you.

We also view religious stories as mythology, which does not mean we think they are untrue. Our Goddess, Nyx, is very real and tangible. Rather, mythology refers to sacred stories intended to instruct and guide people to a spiritual truth through the use of metaphor. Outsiders who read our stories often make the mistake of interpreting them as historical facts, which they are not. Interpreting myths as facts reduces them to something that happened long ago to people who are long dead, and this makes applying their lessons to our own lives much more difficult. Rather, we interpret the stories as myths, where we are intended to find the strength of the hero within ourselves and to see within our own lives the flaws of the villain and take heed that those flaws don't contribute to our own downfall. If we read the myths and apply the lessons to ourselves, learning from the virtues of the teachers and heroes while taking warnings from the tragic flaws of the doomed, then the stories become living traditions and are renewed in every age. Learning from the actions of mythic figures gives us wisdom, for while intelligence is learning from your own mistakes, wisdom is learning from the triumphs and failures of others.

Greek philosophers believed that all things were formed from the elements— earth, air, fire, and water. Add spirit to that and they weren't too far off the mark. Ah . . . I can hear many of you out there protesting, "What about iron and helium, gold and mercury, what about all the elements on the periodic table from hydrogen to unuoctium, should we just chuck all of those and replace them with only five?" While I'm sure many chemistry students would welcome the change wholeheartedly and do a gleeful little dance around the bonfire they created from their partially memorized periodic tables, that is not what I'm suggesting at all. So just wipe that manic grin from your faces and put down the matches.

Remember symbols and metaphors and not taking everything so literally? Well, this is one of those times. The five elements of earth, air, fire, water, and spirit are concepts, categories into which everything can be placed if you look at things symbolically and metaphorically rather than concretely. There are many ways to arrange things. Just as you might arrange the clothes in your closet by color or season, or fat clothes and skinny clothes, all of life can be placed into categories. The periodic table arranges all the elements by their number of protons, their valence electrons, and whether they are metals or non-metals. The children of the earth arrange the elements by their characteristics. Is it rigid and solid? Then it's earth. Wet and flowing? Then it's water. Heat or light equal fire, and abstract or etheric things are air. Iron is a form of earth, while helium, being a gas, is a form of air. Who hasn't seen gold and thought it burned with its own inner fire? And mercury is a form of water; it's the only element that is liquid at room temperature. The characteristics we use in this categorization can be literal, symbolic, or emotional, so the heat of sudden emotional attraction is just as much fire as a pyre and the chilly wash of humiliation as much water as a winter rainstorm.

Elements can also be mutable in almost miraculous ways. An explosive metal, sodium, will combine with the poisonous gas chlorine to make the very earthy salt, and two airs in the form of hydrogen and oxygen gas combine to form the very watery . . . well, water. These transformations are almost magical, but people either don't know about them or don't think about them, so their composition becomes just mundane background information. Think about the magic in your own body, which is a combination of the earth in your bones; muscle and skin kept alive with the air that flows into and out of your lungs; the chemical reactions that provide the fire to warm your blood; the water of life, which flows like a river throughout your being; and lastly the spirit, that spark of deity providing an indefinable power that gives you consciousness and makes you more than just the sum of your parts. The children of earth both see the elements as part of all nature, where everything is a combination of earth, air, fire, and water, and everything from the stones and the trees to the streams and the bunnies has a bit of the divine flowing through it.

In ritual, the children of the earth honor the elements as the primal forces of the universe and as the building blocks of life. Each element is oriented toward a compass point. The pairings of element with direction comes from a time so far back that even the vampyres have no record of their origins, but we believe the associations originated very long ago in the area now known as Great Britain. The east side of what is now England has intense winds that blow in off the channel, so the ancients believed the winds were born in the east. To the south, the further one sails the warmer it gets, so the ancients felt the birthplace of fire was to the south. To the west of England there is the vast expanse of water that is the Atlantic Ocean, which until relatively recently humans believed took you to the very edge of the world, so the ancients felt the west was the home of all water. As one moves north onto the mainland the landscape transforms into mountains so foreboding that few would attempt to pass, so the ancients felt this direction was the very origin of earth. Now, saving the best for last, we have spirit, which is born from within and flows out from the center of our being. Therefore, the center of the Circle is reserved for spirit.

The elements are also represented by the points of the pentagram, which is a five-pointed star. Leonardo da Vinci used the pentagram to represent the head, arms, and legs of his Vitruvian man, and the children of the earth use it to represent the elements—however, while spirit is almost universally associated with the top point, there is a bit of disagreement among the various human groups as to which point represents which of the other elements.

I'll tell you one possibility that I especially like, as its order mirrors the creation of the planet. The spirit point is of course at the top, because everything begins and ends with spirit. Now, when the earth was formed it would have first been a glowing ball churning in a massive inferno of molten elements; therefore, as you trace the pentagram from the top point down and to the right, the first point you encounter is fire. As the inferno began to cool the planet would have begun to take shape, forming a congealed scab over the otherwise blazing interior and giving the first inklings of what this churning sphere was to become, so as the pentagram is traced from the bottom right to the top left the next point that is reached is earth. As the planet cooled, gasses would have been expelled from the heaver elements in a hissing rush of nitrogen, hydrogen, and oxygen, which, along with other gasses, formed the first atmosphere. Therefore, as we trace the pentagram from the upper left to the upper right we next arrive at air. As the planet continued to cool to a point below the boiling point of most liquids, the vapor that had formed from the hydrogen and oxygen mixing in the atmosphere would have started to condense and the first rain would have begun to fall in a torrential down-pour, filling the first oceans and creating the primordial soup from which all life arose. Therefore, as the pentagram is traced from the upper right to the lower left, we encounter the point of water. All things in life are a circle, or at least a cycle, so we finish our pentagram where we began. As our line ascends to the top we again encounter spirit because, of course, everything begins and ends with the spirit.

In addition to being associated with a compass point, each element also has a color that represents it, and in Circle an appropriately colored candle is often used to represent the element. However, before I begin talking about elements and ritual I think I should pause a moment to discuss what Circle is. Circle, for the children of the earth, is a religious service, but not one like many of you will be familiar with. Circles are held for the same reasons all religions hold services and perform rituals. They are held to celebrate sacred times of the year, honor Deity, mark passages (births, weddings, funerals), ask for boons from the Divine (healing, money, or love), and any other reason one might wish to work in conjunction with the Divine. In Circle people stand facing each other, and every person fully participates in the ritual as everyone dances, sings, chants, and experiences the closeness to the Divine that Circle brings. Circles may be performed for a variety of reasons, but each begins by honoring the primal forces of creation—the elements.

For vampyres, Circle begins in the direction of the rising moon, although Wiccans would say it begins with the rising sun, so Wiccans and others associate the eastern quadrant and the element of air with the yellow of that orb. Fire burns with a red/orange flame and embers glow crimson, so the southern quadrant and the element of fire is associated with the color red. Water is blue, and green is the color of the living earth, the grass and trees covering the planet; therefore both the colors for the western and northern quadrants are pretty much self-explanatory. This only leaves spirit as the final element, and what is the color of spirit? There is some debate on this amongst the different groups that comprise the children of the earth. Vampyres and many others use purple as the color of the final element, as it's the highest frequency of light people can discern with their unaided eyes and it's the color of the highest chakra, or energy center, of the body in Hinduism. However, others say spirit is the purity of white absent of all color, or black, since all colors are present within it, or even a blend of the two representing the yin and yang of the soul. Possibly spirit should be the silver and gold of the moon and sun, which many use to represent the Goddess and God. Or perhaps the color of spirit is the palest green of a shaft of light, a bit of fire from the sun after it travels through the air and reflects off a pond covered in water lilies. The experience of spirit is different for every individual and the colors used to represent it can be just as varied and unique.

In ritual, when asking an element to join the Circle, vampyres prefer the person asking to have a special affinity for an element, but such an affinity is not necessary. Wiccans, being human, have less sensitivity for the elemental forces, but with training, even they may be able to call the elements by focusing on the feelings and images associated with each one. When calling the element of air everyone faces east toward the rising moon and, just as Damien does, takes up the yellow candle, lights it, and focuses on everything that exemplifies air. Then Air—the archetypal force that encompasses not only the element but everything that is associated with that element—is invited to join the Circle.

*Guardian of the east, spirit of air, we ask that you bring into our*
*Circle the breath of harmony with all things. Spirit of the air who*
*gives us the breath of life we ask that you come hear us use that*
*breath in song this night.*

The early Greeks considered air to be the first principle of the world, and the Latin word *Spirare*, meaning breath, became the root of our words aspire, inspiration, and even spirit. Air is not simply that which blows; it is the inhalation that infuses our bodies with oxygen down to our tiniest cells. Air is the breath of the Muse that brings inspiration and mental activity. Air is the winds of change, the spoken word, the voice lifted in song or in praise of our Goddess. Air is the arrow that flies, the precise and planned movements of a sword master or a martial artist. It is the breath of a lover on your skin, it is the lips millimeters apart, hovering just beyond each other as your breath mingles and you breathe in the essence of each other in anticipation of a kiss. Birds represent air, as can be seen in the heightened vision of a hawk and in the owl, which represents the wisdom of the goddess Athena, who is still worshipped by Wiccans to this day. Air is represented in a Wiccan Circle by the athame (ceremonial knife), the sword, the pure tones of a bell, and the smoke from incense or a smudge stick, wrapping everyone in its cleansing ethereal tendrils. In fact, a smudge stick or a bell is often carried around the Circle during casting. Air is associated with the zodiac signs of Gemini, Libra, and Aquarius, which are known for their talkative natures and clarity of thought. Look at those who have an affinity for air and you will find that like Damien they will have an agile mind and a quick wit. I have never understood why humans refer to the unintelligent as "air heads," because the domain of the mind is air.

*Guardian of the south, spirit of fire, we ask that you bring the light*
*to our steps. Spirit who kindles the fires of chance we ask that you*
*give us power, exuberance, and dance.*

Fire warms your homes and cooks your food, but it represents so much more in your life. Many consider fire the first tool and the harnessing of fire the turning point between primitive and modern man. The Greeks believed Prometheus stole fire from the gods and gave it to man. Something so powerful being stolen from the heavens so enraged Zeus that he chained Prometheus to a rock and had a vulture rip out and consume his liver daily. Then it would grow back overnight so the process could continue.

The Greeks also divided fire into two kinds of flame—the helpful and the harmful. The helpful kind of fire was that of Hephaestus, god of the smiths, and of Hestia, goddess of the hearth and home fires. The second type of fire was the destructive fire associated with Hades, god of the Underworld. Fires could shift and change from one to the other in an instant, and this same division runs through the fires in our lives, as they can both warm and consume. Passion can become jealousy, caring can become obsession, righteous indignation can transform to blind fury. The warmth of the sun on your body can become painful blisters, and the heat of the body can become a fever that burns the mind. In a Wiccan Circle fire may be represented by a candle, a wand, a staff, or the flame on the smudge stick that transforms the dried herbs into cleansing smoke. A candle is often carried around the Circle to represent the element of fire during casting. In the zodiac the signs Aries, Leo, and Sagittarius, with their energy and enthusiasm, are associated with fire.

Fire is the forceful action that brings victory or defeat, the adrenaline that pushes us to our limits and can drive us over a cliff. Fire fueled Pheidippides' run from Marathon to Athens and melted the wings of Icarus, causing him to plummet into the sea. The goddess Hecate, who is worshipped by many Wiccans today, personifies fire in all its forms: she is known as Pyrphoros (fire bearing), Pyripnon (fire breather), Daidoukhos (torch bearer), and Phosphoros (light bearer).

Fire in any of its forms, whether the warming fire of the hearth, the working fires of the forge, or the fire of passion that ignites the soul, can be a force for creation or destruction. This can be seen in Zoey's Circle, where Shaunee has an affinity for fire. Shaunee is passionate and protective but can get herself into trouble when her passion overrides her reason.

Fire is an element that is invaluable in our lives, but it must be respected, because if you begin to think it's tame, it will bite you just to remind you of its power.

*Guardian of the west, spirit of water, we ask that you allow love*
*to flow into our Circle. Water, the womb that bore all life, we ask*
*that you wash over us cleansing our spirit of toil and strife.*

Water is the waves lapping onto the shore, the soothing beauty of a stream, and the thunder of a waterfall. Water is the dew on the grass, a gentle summer rain, and a snowy winter's day. It is the blood in your veins, the tears you weep, and the sweat on your brow. Water is associated with your emotional nature, your hopes, and your fears. From water we learn to yield and flow, we learn patience and persistence. There is nothing more yielding than water and yet nothing is stronger.

Warriors often revere water. If you strike at it, it's not there—it flows around obstacles and appears behind you. But this ability of water to yield belies its true power, for it can strip a mountain down to a plain, carve giant canyons, and hew a cavern from living rock. Water has the patience to wear away at its opponent little by little; it is called the universal solvent because it will eat away more things than any acid. Water will erode the earth, extinguish fire, and dissolve air dragging it down to the depths of the oceans. In the end water will always win. In a Wiccan Circle, water is often represented by a bowl of water (sometimes salted to purify it and combine it with earth), anything blue, seashells, and the chalice, and water is often sprinkled around the Circle while asking water to join the ritual. The astrological signs of Cancer, Scorpio, and Pisces, with their caring and emotional nature, are associated with water.

The goddess Aphrodite was born from the sea, as indeed all life had its origins in there. Vampyres, Wiccans, and many other religions view water as a cleansing agent and ceremonially immerse, sprinkle, or wash people to cleanse their body, mind, and spirit. The traits associated with water are compassion, caring, wisdom, creativity, compromise, and forgiveness. You can see this in Erin, who has an affinity for water. Erin is very like her "twin" Shaunee, but her personality is not as fiery. She often just flows along with her friend, and is also more willing to compromise and forgive.

> *Guardian of the north, spirit of earth, we ask that you bring to our Circle the peace and security of the earth. Spirit of the earth, from which our very flesh is formed, bring us grounding and stability as our rite is performed.*

From dust we came and to dust we shall return. This concept sounds a bit morbid, but in essence it is correct. We are formed from the earth—well, mainly we are formed from carbon, hydrogen, and oxygen with a few trace elements like calcium to toughen up the bones and iron to give us a bit of color, but when you get right down to it all that is just part of the earth. But what an amazing piece of earth we are, even the humans. (No offense!) We walk, talk, live, and love, all because the spirit moves the earth. But wait, I'm getting a bit ahead of myself; let's jump back to earth.

The earth is often referred to as our mother, because it gives us nourishment, shelters us, and takes us back to her after we pass. All the food we eat, the clothes we wear, and the tools we use ultimately come from the earth. Vampyres revere the earth, and Wiccans and Native Americans, like Zoey's grandmother, view the earth as a living conscious entity that has a spirit of its own. They believe the earth will always take care of us—if we take care of it. We should live in harmony with nature, taking what we need, but only what we need and no more. That we are entrusted as stewards of the earth means we should recycle, replant felled trees, reduce pollution, and minimize our use of fossil fuels whenever possible. The belief is that the earth is a self-healing entity, and if we don't maintain a proper symbiotic relationship with the earth, she will eventually decide we are far too harmful and rid herself of us.

In a Wiccan Circle earth may be represented by the color green or brown, leaves, rocks, or minerals, and salt is often sprinkled around the Circle when asking earth to join the ritual. The astrological signs Taurus, Virgo, and Capricorn, with their practical and responsible natures, are associated with the earth.

The traits of earth are, well . . . down to earth. The archetype of the cowboy who rides the range, sleeps under the stars, and herds cattle is a perfect image for earth, as they are seen to be patient, consistent, and unmovable. Stevie Rae, from her cowboy hat to the boots, and from her small-town upbringing to the natural way she accepts and cares for people, epitomizes the element earth.

The earth is our mother, and when you feel worried or stressed, feel yourself moving down into her. See roots growing from your feet and pulling nourishment and energy into your body. Wiccans refer to this as "grounding," and it will help you find calm, peaceful security when you need it most. Like calls to like, and if you will let it the earth will nurture and protect you. All you have to do is reach out to her, and the earth, your mother, will be there to comfort and protect you, taking away the anxiety and pain so that you can feel calm, secure, and safe in her arms.

*Lord and Lady essence of spirit, we ask that you bring to our*
*Circle the Spirit of love and compassion. Spirit that is our compass*
*for wrong and right lead us through our darkest night.*

The four elements are amazing when you think about them. Air flowing around us infusing not only the sky but also the depths of the sea and the underground hollows with just the proper mix of nitrogen and oxygen to sustain life. Fire from the sun warming this planet to just the right temperature; not so hot that we go all flambé but not so chilly that we shatter. Water covering 75 percent of this planet and hiding mysteries so deep that even we vampyres have yet to discover its secrets. Earth, both the planet and the soil beneath us, the mountains and deserts, all providing homes to the children of this world.

Look again at our bodies, human and vampyre: Air flows through our lungs and fuels the cells of our bodies. Fire manifests in the warmth of our skin. Water makes up 60 percent of our weight and constantly flows both into and out of us, providing the environment for all our bodily functions. Earth makes up our skin, hair, and bone. The four elements combine to form an amazingly intricate machine. But that's all we would be, a squishy golem, an extremely articulate automaton, without one thing—spirit.

The final element, spirit, is the thing that makes us all individuals. Spirit animates us to move beyond a nicely formed but inanimate collection of elements and places us in a position of power and responsibility. Spirit is what brings us joy and sorrow, gives us the ability to love and hate, lets us become enraptured by beauty and makes us despair in depravity. Spirit is our conscience and our compassion, but it is also our anger and pain. Spirit is that tiny fragment of the Divine within us, that piece linking us to the creator. As Shakespeare, who as you know was himself a vampyre, said, "What a piece of work is man, how noble in reason, how infinite in faculties, in form and moving how express and admirable, in action how like an angel, in apprehension how like a god." Zoey, having an affinity for all elements, has to be overwhelmed at times. I imagine that there are times she feels like she is standing in a hurricane while contemplating a rose, all of life swirling around her but still clinging to a bit of beauty that is the Divine.

Spirit gives us the power to think and act, to be caring and compassionate or petty and cruel. Do we feel the exaltation of spirit well within us and marvel at how every person can have their own individual experience of spirit, or do we attempt to force everyone to conform to our own vision of spirit? Zoey chooses to use her gift to help all who are in need to seek understanding and peace, while others use their gift to seek dominance over others. The entire range of vampyre and human emotions are the gift of spirit, but how we choose to use them is entirely up to us.

Circle is opened with a request for the elemental forms of nature to join in the ritual and closed by thanking the elements for their participation in the service. Beginning and ending with the elements is symmetrical, as is the circle itself, and polite, as more of us should be. I mean really, one does not invite someone to join in to something and then not thank them for being there when it's time to leave.

Vampyres feel the song of the elements, but most humans, with a few notable exceptions, seem to consider the immensely awe-inspiring miracle of the elements to be mundane and ordinary. Humans see the life-renewing gift of water freely falling from the sky and complain about how the rain is inconveniencing them. A flower bursts forth from the earth opening its petals to the sun, and a bee dances around it in thanks to the Goddess, while a human contemplates paving over it for a new parking lot. Humans become so wrapped up in their own cleverness that, like Narcissus staring at his reflection, they have become enamored with their own creations. Modern technologic creations have their uses and their place in the modern world, but they are not life; they have no spirit and do not touch our souls. On their side of the looking glass humans have forgotten this and decided that cars are more amazing than horses, buildings more majestic than mountains, amusement parks more desirable than forests, and computer screens more interesting than each other.

There are some exceptions. Wiccans, Native Americans, and other Shamanic people still view the earth as their mother. Wiccans still see the Goddess in all things and view the elements as her elder children, who care for and protect us when we live in harmony with nature and chastise us when we cast nature aside. Of course Wiccans have the advantage of believing that the earth and all of nature is sacred. Like vampyres, they believe the Goddess wove the lessons we are to learn into the very fabric of nature. They believe that there are sacred lessons to be learned in the changing of the seasons, the fall of a raindrop, the rising of the moon, and the budding of a rose. To one who believes the world is our guide, the true meaning of life is found in our relationship to nature, not in our separation from it. If you want to understand the mysteries of nature, watch a caterpillar crawl on a stem, a spider build a web, an eagle soar on an updraft, or a mother hold her child. If you want to experience the Divine look at a mountain, wade into the ocean, or watch the full moon rise (although for humans the sunrise would probably be equally inspiring). If you want to understand yourself, know a deer. I'm not talking about knowing about it or what it eats but knowing why, why a deer, or why anything for that matter. Understand the existence of anything and you will learn something about yourself.

Now, our next discussion will be here next week, when we will talk about the origin of that absurd idea that vampyres turn into bats and fly away.

**BRYAN LANKFORD** is the author of the book *Wicca Demystified: A Guide For Practitioners, Family and Friends*, which seeks to promote a greater understanding of the Wiccan religion by explaining many of the misconceptions about Wiccan beliefs to the public. Bryan is a Wiccan practitioner in the Dallas Pagan community where he lectures extensively about Wicca at colleges and universities, and he has been a guest on both secular and religious radio programs helping people understand the truth about Wicca. Bryan is a member of the Covenant of the Goddess and the Thanks-Giving Square Interfaith Committee, which promotes dialogue and cooperation among people of all faiths.

# { Misunderstood }

## MULTIPLE PARTNERS IN OUR MATRIARCHAL (AND PATRIARCHAL) PAST

*Kristin Cast*

ZOEY REDBIRD takes a lot of crap for having multiple boyfriends. I'm sure, if she were sitting here next to me, she would be pretty upset about being called a slut, a tramp, a whore, and all of the other negative nouns that are thrown at her. I get tons of messages on Facebook from people who make hurtful comments, and I know that our administrative assistant Camden Clark, who keeps up with our House of Night Facebook, MySpace, and email, constantly has to stand up for Zoey. (I do want to point out that, in earlier novels, the guys in Zoey's life should have definitely known about each other. The whole not-being-honest thing doesn't ever go over very well.) My mom and I are often asked when we will make her choose just one guy to be with forever and ever and ever and ever. I can tell you that won't be happening anytime soon. She's a teenager and it's unhealthy for a teen to be focused on one guy and one guy only. Girls shouldn't spend months, weeks, or even days obsessing over boys they won't remember in five years. But, when Zoey is mature and experienced and truly knows herself, she'll pick just one guy . . . maybe.

I say that not only to tease you, but also because within the vampyre society of the House of Night, Zoey doesn't have to choose one mate forever if she doesn't want to. As a High Priestess, she can have a human consort, a warrior, a vamp boyfriend, or any combination of them. In our heavily matriarchal vampyre society, the practice of having multiple partners has been going on for hundreds of years, so it's completely normal!

Shocking, I know, but being in a relationship with multiple partners and having society think it's "normal" isn't some crazy new idea we created for the series. Most people are familiar with the word polygamy, when a man has multiple wives or a woman has multiple husbands—though it's often confused with polygyny, which only addresses a man who has more than one wife. Polygyny has been around for hundreds of years, appearing in many cultures for many reasons. Some factors that might have contributed to the development of polygyny include there being significantly more women than men in a particular society, practical household reasons (women are able to divide tasks in polygynous relationships, and having extra parents around may benefit their children), and plain old egotistical reasons.

Prior to Christian colonization, various African cultures accepted this practice 100 percent (and many countries in Africa still do today, though that acceptance isn't absolute; the controversial Jacob Zuma, who was elected president of South Africa in 2009, has come under heavy criticism in regards to his having three wives).

In places like western Kenya, a man having many wives and children was seen as a symbol of status and wealth, and he could have as many as he could afford. Men had to pay dowries for each wife, so the more wives a man had the more obvious his wealth was to the people in the village. Following old traditions, the current king of Swaziland, Mswati III, has fourteen wives and twenty-three children. And if you think that's excessive, by the time his father King Sobhuza II died, he had amassed seventy wives and over a thousand children!

Polygynous arrangements usually started with what we now think of as a "normal" heterosexual marriage between a man and a woman. The first wife, also called the senior wife, would help her husband look for a second wife if she was getting older and/or needed help meeting household needs such as farmwork, child rearing, and just plain taking care of the husband. Even though the husband could make the decision on his own to find another wife, he would have to consult the senior wife beforehand on things like familial reputation, beauty, values, mental stability, and physical strength. As the senior wife, her position was always respected, and she would always be involved in the addition of subsequent wives. Rarely based on love, the foundations of these marriages instead were based in mutual respect and support. Each spouse's role and status had to be clearly outlined and acknowledged to maintain a harmonious balance, though obviously, this was not always the case as jealousies and power trips understandably resulted in tension.

This way of life changed drastically for many Africans once Christian settlers and missionaries began to arrive on the continent, but don't let their lofty goals fool you. Officially they were monogamous and held the strong belief that God had declared that men were to only be with one wife because "the two," not three, four, or five, "will become one flesh," but they definitely were not innocent. The settlers who came to Liberia came up with something called Chrismonopoly. (Ooooo! Sounds fun! Let's all play!) This hodgepodge of a word is not like your favorite fake-money board game, but if you'd like to play this historic game, go ahead!

The rules:

1. Be a Christian settler.
2. Involve yourself in a monogamous marriage with a Christian wife.
3. (This is the tricky one) While in your monogamous marriage, engage in relationships with native Liberian women.
4. Remember that you're not involved in a polygynous relationship. It's Chrismonopoly!

Umm, yeah right. If it quacks like a duck . . .

The Hebrew bible, the Torah (aka the Old Testament, for Christians), says that polygyny was practiced in ancient Israelite societies and even mentions approximately forty polygynists, including Abraham, Jacob (remember Rachel and Leah?), and, of course, King Solomon. The Torah even includes specific regulations on the practice and states that husbands should make sure that multiple marriages "don't diminish the status of the first wife."

In China, as early as 1911 polygyny was written in the law, but it had actually already been practiced for thousands of years because of the importance their culture places on having children. Emperors could have hundreds, even thousands, of concubines and wives, which would allow for way more kids than simple monogamy. Rich officials and merchants could also have multiple women, thereby increasing their number of children. It was believed that if a man was able to successfully manage not only himself but a family that involved many wives and children, then he would also be able to bring together and manage a nation. Today, polygyny is still practiced in Mainland China, though it was banned there in 1951 under the Marriage Law.

By this time, I bet you're wondering where all the women's rights stuff is and whether or not there's any kind of "poly" dedicated to those with internal genitalia. Well, you're in luck! Polyandry is the term used to describe women who have multiple husbands . . . and lots of patience.

The idea of a polyandrous society was around way before the patriarchal society we are so accustomed to today. In fact, though there's a lot of debate on the issue, scholars such as Edward Hartland, Robert Briffault, and Johann Bachofen believe that most societies were originally matriarchal and matrilineal and even practiced polyandry (though they viewed this as just one of the steps in our evolutionary development toward superior patriarchal societies). Sociologist V. Klein suggests that "in early society women wielded the main sources of wealth; they were the owners of the house, the producers of food, they provided shelter and security. Economically," she points out, "man was dependent upon woman." (You can read a lot more about early matriarchal societies in *When God Was a Woman*, by Merlin Stone.)

These cultural practices may not have lasted in the real world, but you can still see them in many mythologies. In Hindu mythology, Princess Draupadi (she actually had many other names that include Panchali, Parsati, Yognyaseni, and Krishnaa) married five brothers who were known as the five Pandavas. These brothers were not only her husbands, but also acted as bodyguards (or Guardians!), protecting her from anyone who wanted to do her harm. On one occasion, Draupadi was kidnapped, and when her husbands found out, they immediately came to her rescue. Draupadi was amazing. She was said to have grown from the fire out of her father's vengeance against his enemy, and she was known for her beauty, her intelligence, and her eagerness to speak her mind in a man's world. This Indian firecracker has been considered the first feminist in Indian mythology. You go, girl!

Now onto a goddess I'm sure everyone has heard of—Aphrodite. Aphrodite had twelve lovers (though not all at the same time), both mortal and divine. This curvaceous diva of beauty, seduction, love, pleasure, and procreation had a divine consort, Ares, the god of war, as well as a divine husband, Hephaistos. One of the more popular myths about Aphrodite tells of the time she was captured in an invisible net by Hephaistos in the middle of a tryst with Ares. Despite the embarrassment, this event didn't do much to harm Aphrodite's image in the eyes of her fellow gods or worshippers, and I don't think Aphrodite ever received mail about how nasty people thought she was. Mmmhmm. Think about that. She wasn't alone, either. Many other Greek goddesses had multiple lovers and husbands, just as their male counterparts had multiple lovers and wives.

Living a polygamist lifestyle isn't something only gods and goddesses or even people across the pond do, and it's definitely not something that ended a long time ago. It's alive and well, folks. In case you don't have a TV or the internet, or live under a rock, polygamy—or at least polygyny—has made its way onto the boob tube, and not in a very female-friendly way.

From BET to HBO to TLC, our televisions are flooded with images of men with multiple women. Rap music and videos preach and depict that it doesn't only make you a bigger, better, badder man to have a nice car with big rims, but also that it is imperative to be with as many women as possible. Because what woman doesn't want a guy with nice rims, undiagnosed STDs, and a plethora of baby mamas? (Having a kid with a woman may not be marriage, but it's still a long-term commitment.) HBO's *Big Love* depicts a Mormon polygamist family, and producers spent years researching the show's premise to be sure they depicted the fake family's lifestyle fairly and without bias. TLC's new show *Sister Wives* (which I record and watch religiously) follows the real-life activities and drama of a polygamist family and how they handle the addition of a fourth wife.

Much like how the news has desensitized us to violence, our cable televisions have desensitized us to this seriously unbalanced patriarchal practice. Where's our modern polyandry? On an episode of *Sister Wives*, Kody, the husband, and his first wife, Mary, were out to dinner for their twenty-year anniversary. Mary began a conversation about a fourth wife who would soon enter their plural family and the jealousy issues she was dealing with. When she asked him how he would feel if she was giving attention to another guy, Kody was clearly taken aback and responded to her by saying, "Obviously, that's just not something I'm comfortable with imagining. The vulgarity of the idea of you with two husbands, or another lover, sickens me. It seems wrong to God and nature" ("1st Wife's 20th Anniversary," 1-5). Hmm, interesting.

Today, plural marriage—which is the fundamentalist Mormon phrase for polygyny—is practiced among thousands mostly in the United States, Mexico, and Canada. The Church of Jesus Christ of Latter-day Saints (in the United States this is usually the church that people automatically think of when they think about polygamy) says that they totally prohibit plural marriage and have for the past hundred years and "if any of our members are found to be practicing plural marriage, they are excommunicated, the most serious penalty the Church can impose. Not only are those so involved in direct violation of the civil law, they are in violation of the law of this Church." But church law isn't the only law broken in polygamist relationships since they are illegal. Yep, I said illegal, not that the thirty to fifty thousand people who participate actually care since they have an extremely small chance of actually being prosecuted. Well, unless there's evidence of abuse, rape, welfare fraud, or tax evasion.

Though Mormonism prohibits plural marriage, it does acknowledge polygamy. To Mormons, though, it is a divine principle that applies in heaven but is not practiced on earth. Polygamy was first introduced into the faith in the 1830s by Joseph Smith, who was considered God's authorized servant on earth, appointed to "dispense" the gospel to humanity. Smith believed that ancient principles, like polygamy, must be incorporated with new principles, like monogamy. Not all Mormons jumped on board the polygamy train, but many did see value in the practice. Plural marriage was a way to bring them together and give them a distinct identity, allowing them to raise their children to become "righteous seed"—since being raised with a certain belief makes you more likely to commit to it in adulthood. (There's no hope of escaping; you'll definitely turn into your parents.) Plural marriage also ensured that this "righteous seed" would grow into numerous descendants. And for any of you out there who think they do it all for the sex, you're totally wrong. Some Mormon polygamists marry for eternity only, which means that the wife is only on the man's rolls in heaven. It also means that the wife is not allowed to have sex on earth. None. Ever.

There's one modern practice, at least, that's more fair when it comes to having multiple partners, and that's polyamory, which is when people are involved in more than one intimate relationship at a time but are totally open about it. This type of relationship is not only based on love, but also honesty, communication, and trust. The important part is that everyone involved in a polyamorous relationship—whether it's between a man and two (or more) women, a woman and two (or more) men, or any other combination—is okay with it. If so, who are the rest of us to judge?

The House of Night series and Zoey's juggling act have modernized ancient mythology and the history of our species, reaching back to our matriarchal past and using it as a tool to empower women of all ages. I am not asking you to run around being in relationships with multiple men at the same time, or encouraging anyone else to. I just want women to stop judging each other and stand together. If men can pat themselves on the back, so can we.

KRISTIN CAST is a *New York Times* and *USA Today* bestselling author who teams with her mother to write the House of Night YA series. She has stand-alone stories in several anthologies, as well as editorial credits. Currently Kristin attends college in Oklahoma, where she is focusing on attaining her dream of opening a no-kill dog rescue shelter in midtown Tulsa.

# { She Is Goddess }

## GODDESS WORSHIP
## IN THE HOUSE OF NIGHT SERIES

*Yasmine Galenorn*

SHE IS Goddess. She is the moon overhead, full and ripe in the sky. She is the ground under our feet, pungent and ripe with promise. She is the huntress in the woods, fleet of foot, and the washerwoman at the stream, washing bloody garments predicting deaths to come. She wears a triple face: Maiden, Mother, Crone. She is gigantic—the 24,000-year-old Venus of Willendorf, and she is lithe—Eos, the goddess of dawn. She is Kali, she is Artemis and Athena and the Morrigan. As Gaia, the planet, she provides the sustenance that keeps us alive. As Hel, she walks us into the Underworld at our death. Eternal and cyclic, she is Goddess, the primal source of life and death.

Throughout history, the divine feminine has been worshipped and loved, reviled and vilified, adored and feared. She has been exalted, and she has been defiled. As the patriarchal religions rose, the Goddess went from being the soul of the world on which we walked to wearing the face of Eve, who fell from grace and brought down mankind. She began as Lilitu, an ancient and powerful goddess, and was disempowered and twisted into Lilith, a demoness devouring children.

She is every color. She is every size. She is every age. She is life, and she is death. She is also vast—so enormous that no single essay can ever hope to encapsulate her history.

The subject of the Goddess and her worship is so large that, in this essay, I'm going to attempt to narrow down the topic to focus on how P.C. and Kristin Cast have used aspects of Goddess-worship studies—both past and current—to create their own vision of Goddess worship within the House of Night series. We will take a look at various aspects of history and myth, and then examine how they play out in Zoey Redbird's story.

## A FEW DISCLAIMERS

In the interest of full disclosure, I admit that I come at this subject not from an academic standpoint, but from that of a modern Pagan, a priestess, and a shamanic witch. I'm a bestselling author—yes. I also love technology and adhere to a good deal of modern scientific teachings—but in my faith, I'm a shamanic witch. I'm not Wiccan, and I believe in multiple gods/goddesses (most Pagan religions do not view any god as omniscient or omnipotent).

I started as a solitary witch over thirty years ago. I'm self-taught, and eventually went on to lead and work with groups of people. But my personal path has evolved over the years to a very specific focus and, as I did earlier in life, I now prefer a solitary path for most of my workings/rituals, except for certain holidays.

This is the way I choose to practice, but it is not the way all Pagans practice. Among modern Pagans, worship and belief is as variable and flexible as the number of adherents, for most Pagans practice reconstructed versions of what the older rites must have been like—we can never truly know what went on back then.

While it's been suggested in *some* academic circles that there may have been a single worldwide matriarchal Goddess cult, there isn't enough solid evidence to prove this. Thousands of goddesses existed, and even though they often overlapped because of cultural assimilation, each was worshipped and viewed in her own way. However, much of that worship and ritual has been lost through time, and there are so many academic arguments as to the nature of what certain Goddess symbology means that it's an exercise in futility to hope that we can arrive at a clear picture of just how many of the temples/shrines worked, especially those from oral traditions. So we do our best to create new versions of ancient worship for the modern world.

Ask ten different Pagans for a definition of the Goddess and you will get ten different answers. Still, there are a few things that the majority of Pagans believe, and we'll touch on some of those in the following pages.

First, a little background on Goddess worship in general.

## WHEN GODS WERE BORN

As humankind evolved, our survival depended on the ability to read the weather, to follow the herds, and to learn the difference between poisonous and safe plants to eat. Rain, snow, lightning, fire, windstorms—all elements became both adversaries and allies. Without the knowledge of how they worked on a scientific level, we explored them energetically. Our ancestors divined the magical side of the elements—wind, water, fire, and earth—seeing these elements as being sent by the gods or—in some cases—*as gods themselves*.

As religion began to evolve, our ancestors came to believe that our ability to thrive and to survive was dependent on our ability to assuage the whims of these deities and elements. History credits our ancestors with having *created* the gods to fit the world around them, but a number of other Pagans—as do I—take a different view: that our ancestors observed the natural world around them and *discovered* the divinity inherent within that natural order.

And so, the Earth became the Mother, giving birth to animals and plants. Through her nurturing the people survived. When she was angry and turned her breast away, the people starved. Sacrifices were made to her in hopes for her lenience, and celebrations were held to rejoice and thank her during the bountiful times. Holidays arose, correlating with the equinoxes, solstices, and, eventually, the cross-quarter days. Between the Sun (male) and the Earth (female), the circular Wheel of the Year evolved—which modern Pagans still celebrate. Life was seen as a circle—from birth to life to death to birth again, and as the wheel of the year turned, so did the wheel of life, ever upward in a spiral.

## The Spiral Path in the House of Night

In the House of Night series, we see the spiral on the uniforms of the Third Formers at the House of Night, where it represents following the path of night to learn the ways of the goddess Nyx. The symbolism of the spiral can be seen in many forms within Paganism and Goddess worship in the real world, as well. In addition to representing Triple Goddess worship, it can represent the path to the inner self, the spiral of life, the helix of DNA, and the concept of reaching from the inner core to the outer universe, and is also linked to the womb and fertility rites.

The concept of the living earth as a goddess is more than just a concept to those of us who actively follow Paganism as a spiritual path. This belief celebrates life and acknowledges the place of death in the cycle. Light and shadow are balanced—without one, the other cannot survive. These beliefs combine the carnal and the cerebral and the spiritual.

For a time, the Goddess was forced underground, though she remained very much alive. For centuries, Pagans were forced to sublimate their beliefs, hiding them in the guises of monotheistic holidays and as superstitions. For any religion that is patriarchal in nature has no place for the divine feminine *if she is given an equal stature to the God.* But in most Neo-Pagan circles today, Paganism and Goddess-worship revere the divine feminine on an equal level with the divine masculine. In most cases, one gender does not subjugate the other. And so we come to the role of the priest and the priestess.

## THE PRIESTESS AS SERVANT

The Goddess worship within the House of Night Series is a matriarchal sort. There are priestesses, but no priests, although there are special roles for male vampyres, as with the Sons of Erebus. In this, as well as the rituals we see performed by high priestesses (and high priestesses in training) in the series, including Zoey and Neferet, the Casts' series mirrors modern Pagan roles and rites more than it mirrors the past duties of priesteshood.

Historically, priests were as important to their gods and goddesses as were priestesses and, in most Pagan circles, are equally honored today. But what did these ancient priests and priestesses do in their positions? And how did the modern role of the priestess evolve?

First and foremost, the priestess served her goddess. Again, with so many different temples and gods and beliefs, there can be no single answer as to how priestesses served—no "correct" choice to this multiple choice test.

Among her sacred duties, a priestess might: conduct rituals in worshipping her goddess, see to temple business, act as sacred harlot, go to war, heal the sick, tend to the hungry, or prepare the dead for their journey into the afterlife. One of the most famous rituals (which stretched across several cultures but came into play heavily with Celtic legend and lore) was that of the *heiros gamos*.

In numerous Pagan religions—though perhaps best known in the Celtic realms—the heiros gamos (a Greek term meaning sacred marriage of a god and goddess) was mirrored in the marriage of the king to the land. The land was personified as a goddess of sovereignty—a goddess who held power over a certain area or people. The would-be king underwent a series of exhausting physical trials to test if he was fit to be king, but once decreed suitable, the aspirant king would then undergo ritual sex with a priestess representing the local goddess of sovereignty in order to finalize his marriage to the land. This would solidify the king's loyalty to his people and the land over which he ruled and was a binding oath.

In modern Paganism, the priestess (and/or priest) facilitates rites during celebrations and rituals. She keeps the energy flowing smoothly, focuses the magic being raised, takes care of anyone disrupting the Circle, and basically leads the rituals—much of what we see in the House of Night series. In some traditions, the priestess will channel the goddess being served, and together with the priest will at times reenact the heiros gamos ritually, using a blade (representing the phallus of the god) and chalice (representing the womb of the goddess). During the ritual, the blade is lowered into the chalice as a representation of sexual union.

Not all priestesses today follow a single goddess or even a named goddess. A number—especially within the Wiccan tradition—follow what might be termed the generic "Earth Mother" or "Moon Goddess." And then there are many priestesses—like myself—who are pledged to either a specific god or goddess, or group of gods. But modern Pagans almost always work out a personal connection with the gods: what they want us to do and what we need to do for them.

In the House of Night series, we explore the concept of Goddess worship through the eyes of Zoey Redbird. Her path follows a traditional modern high priestess's path: she is chosen by her Goddess, undergoes her first ritual, and begins her training toward the goal of becoming high priestess. As with priests and priestesses of old, she is her Goddess' agent in the world, acting on her behalf and communicating her wishes. But that is not the only role Zoey can be seen as playing within the House of Night series. And it is here that we move into an examination of one of the more prevalent perceptions of the Goddess, the Triple Goddess, and how the three faces of the Goddess are reflected by characters within the series.

## THE TRIPLE FACE OF THE GODDESS

One common motif in the history of Goddess worship shows the Goddess as having three faces—Maiden, Mother, and Crone. She rules all aspects of women's lives, and many goddesses around the world were seen as having a triple face (Brighid from Celtic mythology, Hecate from Greek mythology, and the Morrigan from Irish mythology, for example).

Probably the best-known example of the Triple Goddess is the Fates—three sisters spinning out the destiny of humans. The Moirae—three Greek goddesses—were said to spin out each mortal's web of life on a loom. Their parents were thought to be either the Goddess Nyx (the primal goddess of night), or Zeus (the leader of the Greek gods) and Themis (one of the Titans).

The Maiden Goddess spins the life-thread, the Mother measures it out, and the Crone cuts it: Clothos, Lachesis, and Atropos, respectively, in the Greek tradition. And so we see the powers of the Triple Goddess encapsulated by the Fates—youth, the prime of life, and age.

## The Fates in the House of Night

In a nod to the Triple Goddess, P.C. and Kristin include a silver silhouette of the Fates on the Sixth Formers' uniforms. The symbol even includes Atropos' scissors, to signify the end of the students' time at the House of Night—or the end of their life, if they don't complete the Change.

The three faces of the Goddess also correspond to the life cycle of womankind, which acts as a mirror of the divine feminine within mortal woman.

### The Maiden

In her Maiden aspect, the Goddess is the fleet-footed nymph of the woodland; she is the huntress, unencumbered by children or entanglements. As she explores her life, she discovers her strengths and callings. A woman under the Maiden phase is still free, unclaimed by man. Though she may have a man by her choosing, she will not have a mate yet.

## The History of the "Virgin"

The word "virgin" comes from the Greek/Latin word "virgo," which means "maiden." Originally, sexuality was not an aspect of the word. Virgin was, in fact, a term of power, applied to women who lived "apart" from men. The definition did not necessarily only include women who hadn't had sex. It referred to women who were not bound to a brother, father, or husband. Only later did the word "virgin" take on a sexual meaning and, as has happened often in history, reduced a woman's power to the state of her genitals.

During the Maiden phase, women explore their lives and decide the path upon which they wish to walk. This is an invaluable time, allowing for experimentation and education. Unfettered by children, the Maiden is free to travel, to go to college, to begin building a career, to decide whether she wants to be a mother or not.

In her full power, the Maiden is sexuality beckoning but not fully realized; she is strong in body and only at the beginning of realizing her full potential. She is painting her self-portrait, but there are pieces missing because she has yet to experience them.

## The Mother

As the Goddess moves into her Mother phase, fertility and creativity emerge. The Earth Goddess was generally portrayed at her most fertile, with a huge rotund belly, large breasts, and strong thighs—the Venus of Willendorf is the most famous statue thought to represent the Earth Mother.

Women coming into the Mother cycle had children. This was, for the most part, a given. Until the modern age, most birth control methods (except for abstinence) were chancy at best. Therefore, if you were female and you had sex, it was a fair bet you'd end up pregnant, sooner or later. Women were revered for their ability to give life: to bring forth life was a sign of divinity. Women were touched by the Goddess.

So the Mother Goddess signified creativity, fertility, and nurturing. The Mother was the goddess of the harvest—the queen of bounty to sustain the people through the long winters. She became Mother Bear, protecting her cubs; Ocean Mother, bringing in the treasures of fish and shellfish; she was symbolized by Cow—another fertility symbol—and by Rabbit.

Modern women entering their Mother phase have many more options than just bearing children to explore their fertility and creative energies. Nurturing a career and/or a partner (be it a man or woman) also falls under the Mother aspect. Women ripen fully into their sexuality during this phase—what began as experimentation during the Maiden phase now blossoms into the woman who knows what she wants, in the bed or out of it.

Women who fully embrace their Mother phase and release the Maiden stage without regret grow in personal power and confidence. They evolve into the Queen, not afraid of their age, not afraid of society and her whims. They nurture themselves along with their families and their friends. They protect. They defend the home and hearth, as well as their positions.

## The Crone

When we turn to the Crone, in our society we often think of an ugly old woman who has no voice, no sensuality left, and no impact on society, but that is far from the truth in Goddess worship and modern Paganism. The Crone embodies wisdom and power. She understands compassion, but her methods often involve tough love—the love that lets the mentee learn the consequences of making wrong choices, the love that will protect from harm but will not coddle. The Crone is objective and understands the nature of balance—that without shadow, we cannot have light. Without sorrow, we cannot fully understand joy.

She is still sexual, but because the possibility of pregnancy has faded, she can enjoy her passion without worry. She is freer than either the Maiden or the Mother with her sexuality. If she is outside of a monogamous relationship, she can pick and choose her lovers as she will.

The Crone is firmly established in her career and her life path. She is a force to be reckoned with. Spiritually, the Crone embodies the Dark Mother. She is closer to death than her two companions, and she rules over the Underworld in many of her guises. As we saw earlier, she is the Fate who cuts the life-thread for each mortal.

The Crone is close to her magic. She has had longer to practice—she's learned her strengths and built upon them. She works under the Dark Moon, and her magic is that of stars and the deep woodland and the veil that separates the worlds of life from the worlds of spirit.

The Crone cleanses the land, she is the wildfire that clears the scrub, she is the avalanche that sheds unbalanced snow banks, she peels away the scab to expose the new, healthy skin. And she also reveals hidden secrets and ugly truths so that spiritual cleansing can take place.

As she moves toward the veil, the Crone begins to shed her ties to the world; she walks the path to the Underworld, knowing that it is simply another transformation. In Paganism this journey is known as the Eternal Return—death leads to life leads to death leads to life again, and on and on.

## THE FACE OF THE TRIPLE GODDESS WITHIN
## THE HOUSE OF NIGHT SERIES

While the Triple Goddess is referenced only indirectly in the House of Night series, we can still find clear expressions of the Maiden, Mother, and Crone aspects within the books.

Zoey Redbird is the Maiden—young, learning her place in the vampyre world, discovering her new abilities and potentials. She dates, but she isn't tied down to any one man yet. She is in training, someday looking at being High Priestess, but for now, she's got a long way to go and has questions, doubts. She makes the wrong choices at times and is beginning to learn through her mistakes.

At least at first, Neferet serves as a mother figure for Zoey and for the rest of the House of Night, as she ostensibly is there to guide and nurture the fledglings as they learn to live their new lives. In her role as High Priestess, Neferet also serves as spiritual advisor, as the voice of Nyx, and as the guardian of the gates of death for the fledglings who don't make it through the Change.

Sylvia Redbird—Zoey's grandmother—can be seen as the Crone. She is the fount of wisdom, the elder who has seen great dangers before in her life. She is both resource and support, and yet she can also employ tough love when necessary: she turns her own daughter away when she sees her head down the wrong path, and supports her granddaughter instead.

But the powers of each life phase can corrupt. Neferet lets her desire for power overwhelm her duty to use that power responsibly and commits what could conceivably be the one "sin" common to most belief systems: overstepping the boundaries of her position and assuming she can challenge the Goddess to which she was bound. In essence, she perverts the words of her Goddess in order to strengthen her own position. She twists Nyx's power and, therefore, Nyx chooses someone else—in this case Zoey—to be her mouthpiece. But as of this point in the series, Zoey, still in her Maiden phase, has not gained enough power to challenge Neferet.

Aphrodite was the Maiden, but she also abused her power as leader of the Dark Daughters and was cast out. Nyx does not turn her away fully, but instead presents her with new struggles as Aphrodite seeks to relearn her place within the order. As she discovers more of her compassionate self and grows into her role as Nyx's prophet, Aphrodite begins to enter the Mother phase—now human, but still a mirror of the Goddess. As her character develops a conscience and she begins to know what it's like to actually care for others, she enters her nurturing phase.

## OTHER FACES OF THE GODDESS IN
## THE HOUSE OF NIGHT SERIES

While the Triple Goddess is one of the best-known facets of the Goddess, they are not the only way of envisioning her, and we can also find other aspects of her within the series. First, there is the Bright Mother/Dark Mother duality. Here, bright and dark do not necessarily represent good and evil (just as light and dark do not in the House of Night series), but what essentially equates to the Shadow Self and the Outer Self. The Bright Mother is compassionate, nurturing, and looks after her children. One can turn to her for a shoulder to cry on, a companion with whom to celebrate. She is joyous and mirthful, and filled with hope and optimism. The Dark Mother is the shadow—she is the force of justice. She may have compassion but she will not show mercy; she is the defender and protector of wronged women and children in peril. We turn to the Dark Mother when we need to reveal hidden secrets, to strengthen our will and call upon our inner warrior woman.

We can see these dual aspects of the Goddess within the striking case of Stevie Rae Johnson, whose journey reminds me of that of Persephone, Queen of the Underworld, who lives half the year in the Underworld and half the year in the world above.

Stevie, like Persephone, starts out a young innocent maiden. She is marked for the Change, but instead of following the Triple Goddess journey, she is carried into the Underworld, where she essentially becomes queen of the red fledglings. (Neferet plays the part of Hades, who steals her away.)

Stevie Rae's power grows as she transforms, and she can no longer be considered a Maiden, but even though she watches over the red fledglings, she's not necessarily the "bright mother." She has been cast into her power early, and so instead becomes the "dark mother" and the new red vampyres' elder matriarch.

Where Persephone journeys into the light for six months of the year, so Stevie "returns" to herself enough to spend part of her time with her old friends—but she will never be the same. She now belongs in the Underworld, and must learn to balance her light and dark sides—the Bright Mother warring with the Dark Mother—and accept both.

## THE GODDESS AND THE MOON

Another aspect of Goddess worship that we cannot ignore within the series is that of the Moon Goddess. The Goddess has long been connected with the moon, as well as the Earth. Correlations were noticed between the menstrual cycle and the moon's cycle as far back as ancient Assyria, and woman's monthly bleeding was first seen as holy. The power to bleed without a visible wound, without being harmed by that bleeding, could only be a powerful magical force. Eventually, as patriarchal religions rose in power and sought to sublimate the feminine sex and strength, this magical power became frightening. Women were often sequestered during their cycles and required to undergo ritual cleansing before returning to daily lives.

*The Sabbatu*

In ancient Assyria, rituals were performed on the new moon and on the seventh, fourteenth, and twenty-first days of the moon's cycle. This directly paralleled not only the moon's orbit around the Earth, but also the twenty-eight-day menstruation cycle. The word Sabbat—used in Pagan rites to denote holidays, and the word Sabbath—used in Judeo-Christian faiths—both have their origins in the word "sabbatu," which is associated with these Assyrian cyclic rituals.

Since the night is associated with the moon, so were dreams, intuition, visions, passion, and the wild, feral side of the forest. A number of the goddesses are connected with the moon in one phase or another. Most goddesses of the Hunt are connected with the moon (Diana, Artemis, Mielikki), as are powerful goddesses of magic (Hecate, Cerridwen, Arianrhod, Aradia).

Magic performed in connection with the moon is timed to correlate with the aspects of both the phase of the moon and the goddesses associated with that particular phase.

The Waning Phase (as the moon moves toward the new moon) and the new moon are the best times in which to perform binding magic and scrying magic (magically divining for information using tarot cards, a scrying mirror, the surface of water, or even meditation). This is also a good time in which to magically release things no longer needed.

During the Waxing Phase (as the moon grows toward full and the full moon), we practice magic to strengthen new beginnings and new projects, encourage personal growth, bring culmination to projects already started, empower creativity, and encourage health, prosperity, and materialization. As the moon grows, so does our magic.

While Nyx isn't necessarily a goddess of the moon—either in the House of Night series or in actual mythology—she *is* a goddess of the night, and she reflects many aspects of the moon goddesses. We can see this connection in the visions she gives Aphrodite—and in Zoey's dreams. Her rituals are performed at night, under the moon, and the vampyres over whom she rules live and function at night, rather than in the daylight.

Nyx might easily be considered a goddess of both dark and light moons (and not all moon goddesses were connected with both phases)—for she offers hidden secrets that are associated with the dark moon, and yet her rituals are held under the full moon, and sexuality—connected with the full moon—is an implied part in both general vampyre mythos and the House of Night series. Think of Zoey's reaction to blood, or the sensuality in the Full Moon Ritual Neferet performs in *Marked* (or Aphrodite's less refined bump-and-grind version).

Nyx's association with the moon is also shown in the series through the triple moon necklaces worn by the members of the Dark Daughters and Sons. Its depiction of the waxing crescent, the full moon, and the waning crescent is frequently used as a symbol of the Goddess.

## THE CASTS' GODDESS

Though the particular combination of rituals, practices, and beliefs the Casts have created is unique to the House of Night series, it pays homage to many aspects of modern Pagan goddess worship. The Casts have taken a goddess of myth and fleshed her out for their fictional world, and they have done the same for her followers. They have created an alternative universe where a Goddess looms high over the night—where priestesses walk the world in the robes of vampyres, honoring the Goddess in worship as in old legends, and practices are brought into the modern day.

As I said in the beginning, the Goddess is alive and well; she has been here from the beginning of the world and will be here until Earth takes her last breath. Through real-world worship and fictional worship, she has been honored and revered down through time. And the Casts' world and series fit snugly into her library of legend and lore.

*New York Times* and *USA Today* bestselling author YASMINE GALENORN writes two bestselling urban fantasy series: the Otherworld series (aka Sisters of the Moon series) and the Indigo Court series, for Berkley Publishing and Berkley Jove Publishing. In the past, she wrote the Chintz 'n' China series—a paranormal mystery series—for Berkley Prime Crime; the Bath and Body series—a short-lived mystery series (under the name of India Ink)—again for Berkley Prime Crime; and eight metaphysical nonfiction books on the subjects of witchcraft, tarot, sex magic, and totem magic for Llewellyn Publications and Crossing Press. A modern Pagan and shamanic witch, she lives in Kirkland, Washington, with her husband, Samwise, and their cats. Yasmine considers her life a mixture of teacups and tattoos (the former in her china hutch, the latter on her skin), and can be found on the web at www.galenorn.com.

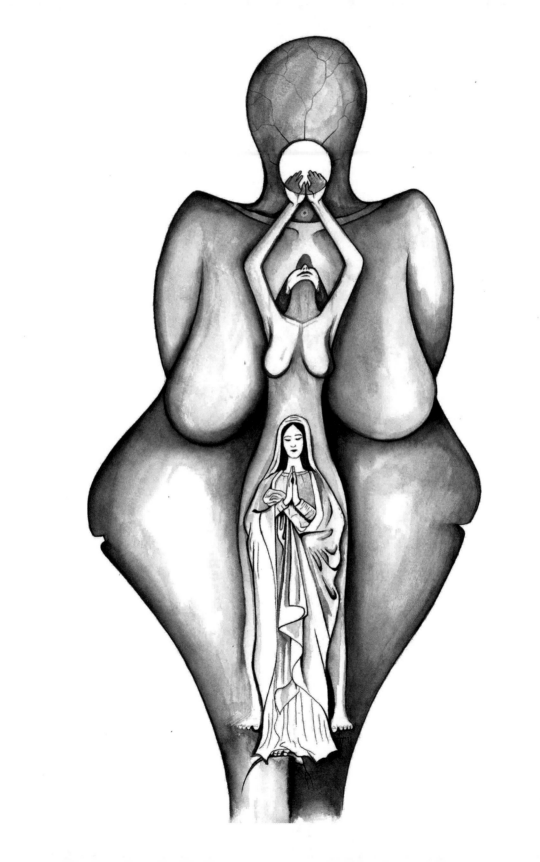

# { Worshipping the Female Deity }

*Christine Zika*

BEFORE I was P.C. Cast's editor on her Goddess Summoning romances, I once worked with three female mystics on a self-help book for women. During one of our conversations, the authors pointed out that a lot of church rituals—burning incense, the use of flowers, and candle-lighting—had origins in Pagan and polytheistic traditions.

Now, I'm Greek Orthodox, a branch of Christianity similar to Catholicism that is heavy on tradition, ritual, and symbolism. So while I take pride in my faith, I also take pride in my ethnic roots, which stretch back to the ancient Greeks and their beliefs in the gods and goddesses of Olympus. When I worked with P.C., I was always amused when she would call or write to me and address me as "Goddess Editor." Each of the books in the Goddess Summoning series (*Goddess of the Sea, Goddess of the Rose, Goddess of Love*, etc.) revolved around an everyday woman who is transformed when one of the mythical goddesses enters her life and helps her find love, and I assumed P.C.'s title for me was a play on the series. But as I've gotten to know her over the years and as I've read through each of the House of Night books, I realize that for P.C. the idea of worshipping the female deity is deeply entrenched, touching her personal, professional, and emotional life.

P.C. brings the light and mysticism of the female deity she so loves into the House of Night series. We see the Goddess in her rendering of the omnipresent Nyx, and in all of her strong female characters—both good and evil—like Zoey, Stevie Rae, and Neferet. But more importantly, we also see the divine female in the Christian figures of Sister Mary Angela and the Benedictine nuns.

## THE WOMEN OF THE HOUSE OF NIGHT

We are first introduced to the benevolent Christian element in *Untamed*, the fourth book in the House of Night series. Here, Aphrodite and Zoey visit the Street Cats rescue shelter to volunteer. When they arrive, they are surprised to see that the shelter is run by nuns and are further floored when one of them, Sister Mary Angela, remarks that she thinks cats are spiritual creatures.

At this point, Zoey's experience with Christianity has been strongly influenced by her stepfather's affiliation with the hate-mongering, narrow-minded People of Faith. Naturally, she is wary of trusting anyone too religious, but as she interacts with the nuns she tries to avoid falling into the same intolerant trap. (Aphrodite is a harder sell, willingly laying blame on Christianity for past cat killings due to witch connections.) The more Zoey talks with Sister Mary Angela, the more she realizes that women, by nature and instinct, have a spiritual connection with each other. With compassion and empathy as her guides, the wise woman can see beyond what male-propagated belief systems deem good and evil.

As the conversation between the girls and the nuns continues, Zoey and Aphrodite's preconceptions are further disproved. The nuns remain unfazed after finding out the girls are vampyre fledglings. Sister Mary Angela even goes so far as to offer to pray for the soul of Loren Blake, the House of Night's recently deceased poet laureate. Still, Zoey is skeptical. Don't the nuns believe she and the other fledglings are doomed to hell because they worship a goddess?

Sister Mary Angela responds, "Child, what I believe is that your Nyx is just another incarnation of our Blessed Mother, Mary." And so the convergence of the religions begins here, with the simple belief that a female deity watches over all her children, Christian *and* Pagan.

Sister Mary Angela adds, "I also believe devoutly in Matthew 7:1, which says 'Judge not, that ye not be judged,'" crystallizing one of the simplest and most important tenets of Christianity: *Love thy neighbor as yourself.* Love each other. Pray for each other. Regardless of race, religion, or ethnicity, we are all people sharing the same earth and we must all help each other. Our differences are less important than all we have in common.

In the House of Night, everyone has access to the Goddess, though they may call her by different names. The rituals they use to reach her, however—like the rituals we use in our world, whether we are Christian, Pagan, or other— have as many similarities as they do differences.

## THE GODDESS AND THE VIRGIN

At the center of the Pagan traditions in the House of Night is Nyx, Goddess of the vampyres. Born out of Chaos, she was among the first of the Greek gods and existed beyond rule. Not even Zeus, father of the Olympians, reigned above her.

The Virgin Mary is younger than Nyx, but surrounded by as much mysticism as the Goddess of primordial night. Chosen to bear the son of God through the Holy Spirit, Mary is highly revered in most sects of Christianity, second only to the Holy Trinity (God, Jesus, and the Holy Spirit). While she may be referred to as Saint Mary, she is considered a higher power, especially in the Catholic and Eastern Orthodox faiths.

Historically, practitioners of Christianity and Paganism have often been at odds, a fact evidenced by such bloody confrontations as the 200-year Holy Crusades and the Salem Witch Trials. But despite the centuries of bad blood between these religious traditions, their primary female deities share quite a few characteristics.

In particular, Nyx and Mary are linked through motherhood.

## THE DIVINE MOTHER

Numerous fertility goddess artifacts found around the world have led many to speculate that the worship of the female deity is older than that of masculine gods. Not too surprising when you think about what is at the core of the female deity's identity: the power to create life. Everything on this earth has a starting place, a beginning, and it is the female members of most earth species that have been gifted with the power to give birth. While Nyx and Mary also share this gift, they do so in exceptional ways.

The Virgin Mary was the only child of an old and barren couple. Her birth was a miracle to her parents, and for this miracle they pledged Mary's service to the church. When she was still a young girl, they betrothed her to the carpenter Joseph, but the angel Gabriel visited Mary and gave her the news that she would bear the Son of God through immaculate conception. Devoted to God and the church, Mary accepted this news willingly.

The subsequent conception and deliverance of the Savior of mankind made Mary one of the most celebrated figures in Christianity, particularly in the Greek Orthodox tradition. I have never been to a Greek Orthodox church in the United States or abroad where an icon of the Virgin Mary holding the baby Jesus was not prominently and reverently displayed. August 15th, the feast day of the Assumption that marks the Virgin's death and passing into heaven, is celebrated as a high holiday with fanfare equal to Christmas (the beginning of her son's life) and Easter (the celebration of her son's resurrection from death).

Like Mary, the Nyx of Greek myth was also known for autonomous birth and may just be one of the first women to ask, "Who needs a man?" Though often linked to her consort Erebus, with whom she had children, Nyx gave birth to the majority of her progeny on her own. Hypnos (sleep), Oneira (dreams), Charon (ferryman to death), the Fates (the Moirae and the Keres), the Hesperides, Nemsis (retribution), Apate (deception), Philotes (friendship), Geras (age), and Eris (strife) were all born without male intervention. How's that for sisters doing it for themselves?

## FEMALE WORSHIP

The amazing power of fertility as exhibited by Nyx and Mary forms the basis of most worship of the female divine. Associated with fertility are realms of nature, the hearth, and the home. In fact, most of the well-known female deities in ancient and contemporary polytheistic and monotheistic religions—Gaia, Isis, Kali—rule over common elements of earth, the household, fertility, love, and internal energy. It is to these female deities that humans have turned to when praying for families, loved ones, and homes.

In the House of Night series, female worship and ritual is marked strongly by compassion, reliance on instinct, and an innate connection to the elements: air, fire, water, earth, and spirit. Coloring all of these things is perhaps the strongest universal element of all: the encompassing love and protection offered by the female divinity.

As the female deity watches over all her children, her children have the faith that when they call on their Goddess through prayer and ritual she will come to their aid. Several times, we see Zoey calling out to Nyx for help, and Nyx often answers her through the protective element of Spirit. Not only does Zoey believe that the Goddess will protect her, she believes that her control over the elements, a gift from Nyx, will see her through danger, a belief echoed by the rest of Zoey's circle. We see, too, that even when her followers stray to the side of darkness, Nyx always gives them a chance to return to the light.

Zoey's trust and faith in Nyx is not at all unlike the faith Christian practitioners place in Mary, mother of saints. The familiar image of the Virgin holding the child Jesus close to her bosom is symbolic not only of a mother protecting her child, but that of the archetypal Great Mother protecting all her children. In the Greek Orthodox religion, one can call on any of the saints for protection or assistance, but the one called upon most in times of panic is the Virgin Mary. In Greek, the most common phrase used is *Panaghia Mou*, or "My Saint-of-All." (As the woman who bore the Savior, Mary ranks above all the saints.) And as with Zoey's pleas to Nyx, it matters less what you do in praying to Mary than the intent in your heart when calling upon her.

## PRAYER CANDLES AND CIRCLE RITUALS

However, in reaching out to the divine, it seems too simplistic to just call out to them. Our base instincts require rituals and formalities, including prayers and offerings that illustrate our needs and devotion. And in many Christian traditions, those practices are not all that different from the ways we see the House of Night vampyres reach out to Nyx, or from religious practices in other cultures.

When I go to church, the first thing I do is light a candle. I make a wish for myself and for the well-being of my loved ones, and in front of an icon, usually the Virgin Mary holding the baby Jesus, I pay my respects by crossing myself, saying a prayer, and kissing the icon. In addition to lighting a candle, my mother always makes a point to cut a rose or some fresh basil from her garden and lay it at the icon's base. In Roman Catholic churches, there is usually a basin or wall fixture filled with holy water nearby in which worshippers can dip their fingers before crossing themselves.

Wiccans follow a similar tradition when they cast a spell—or an organized wish, as my female mystic writers have explained it to me. Set up your altar, light a candle, offer flowers to the deity, and make a wish.

In Nyx's circle, we see these same elements represented and called forth in a different way. With colored candles in hand, the House of Night fledglings take their places at the north, south, east, and west points of the circle, place-ments that also evoke the sign of the Christian cross: the father (top/forehead), the son (bottom/heart), and the holy spirit (left and right/the shoulders). The circle caster then lights each fledgling's candle, acknowledging the corre-sponding element and welcoming it into the circle: yellow air (evoking the smoke rising from the Christian votive candle), red fire (the candle's flame), green earth (the flowers and basil at the icon's base), blue water (the blessed holy water with which worshippers cross themselves), and purple spirit (the wish/prayer we send to the deity).

In the House of Night series, candle use is not limited to circles, though; in the series, we also see these wax pillars serving as a means of protection. When the Raven Mockers begin to manifest on the House of Night campus in *Untamed*, Grandma Redbird comes to stay with Zoey, bringing with her tools drawn from Cherokee tradition for Zoey's physical and spiritual protection. They hang a dream catcher in the window, but they also light a moon candle to keep Kalona away.

Every Saturday night and Sunday morning during religious holidays, my grandmother and mother would set out a small glass covered with a special dome with a cross on it and fill it with oil. Like Zoey's moon candle, lighting the wick of the oil candle was a way of bringing God into our home and protecting us through the day and night. If you travel in Greece, you will notice small stands—stone columns with single stone boxes on top—by the side of highways, especially in the more rural areas. On each stand is a little door with a cross on it, and inside is an icon and a small glass filled with oil. Nightly, an older village woman will fill the glass with oil and light it. Now these stands seem to have been around forever. I'm not quite sure why they were built or how or when the trend took off, but I suspect that before cars became such a common convenience, when people were still traveling difficult mountainous regions by mules or by foot (not that long ago, think 1940s), they wanted to see a light on a dark road. A sense that someone was watching over them. A place where they could stop and say a prayer:

*Panaghia Mou, My Virgin, watch over me and my family. Keep us safe.*

## SPIRITUAL CLEANSING

The cleansing rituals in the House of Night series, too, are similar to spiritual cleansing rituals in some Christian religions.

In Cherokee religion, smudging has been used for centuries for rituals involving cleansing, purifying, or protection. Burning a bundle of herbs (usually sage) and wafting the smoke over the body was a way of honoring the Great Spirit and cleansing the individual's spirit. In *Untamed*, when Zoey calls Grandma Redbird for advice on Aphrodite's vision prophesying the return of Kalona, Grandma Redbird advises they each do a cleansing ritual before she will allow Zoey to explain her situation: "Zoey, I'm going to light the smudge pot before we speak any more of these creatures. I'm using sage and lavender. I'll be fanning the smoke with a dove's feather while we talk. Zoeybird, I suggest you do the same." The herbs in Grandma Redbird's smudge pot are the same ones Zoey uses to correct and chase away the evil spirits Aphrodite accidently calls during her disastrous Samhain ritual in *Marked*.

The ancient Greeks and Romans, as well as the Babylonians, did something very similar in their religious cleansing and purification ceremonies: they burned incense. Incense also plays a role in Chinese culture. During religious events in ancient China, according to historian Joseph Needham, "the incense-burner remained the centre of changes and transformations associated with worship, sacrifice, ascending perfume of sweet savour, fire, combustion, disintegration, transformation, vision, communication with spiritual beings, and assurances of immortality."

In Catholic and Eastern Orthodox practices, incense is burned ritualistically during regular and special prayer services and Masses in something called a censer. A censer, which hangs from chains, is a vessel shaped like cup or a bowl. The censer is surrounded by twelve small bells (to symbolize Christ's twelve apostles) and contains little carbon discs that are set on fire. Incense is placed on the carbon disks and the censer is then swung toward icons and worshippers with the purpose of helping prayers travel to Heaven.

Incense burning is also used in household spirtual cleansing rituals. In my home growing up and even still today, my family has a tiny vessel (not a censer, more like a brass holder) that we use to burn incense. We regularly walk around the house with it and make the sign of the cross in front of doors and windows. This is a mode of cleansing intended to banish negative energy, much like the Wiccan and Cherokee use of a smudge stick. Grandma Redbird, I think, would approve.

## GIVING THANKS

There is one other element I'd like to touch on here, one that is common across almost all religions: gratitude. For everything we receive from our deities, we must be thankful.

When we ask and receive, there must be a show of appreciation: a mental and verbal acknowledgment of "thank you."

Zoey understands this intimately. Through the love of her friends and with the help of Nyx, Zoey, almost killed and left with a ragged scar from a Raven Mocker, is healed and becomes whole again. Afterwards:

> I lifted my hand, letting my fingers run across my throat. Nothing. There was not a scratch there. I closed my eyes and sent a silent thank you for my friends' prayer to Nyx. (*Untamed*)

Giving thanks is a big part of the vampyre religious tradition. We only have to look as far as the closing of the circle ritual in which Zoey thanks each element before releasing it back into nature. And Christians also believe in giving thanks in acknowledgement of divine gifts. Even things as simple as a meal are acknowledged at the dinner table. This is why we say grace.

By thanking our god or goddess, we are performing the same ritual, whether we do so with prayer, with flowers, with sacrifice, with an oath, or with a promise of change. But above all, every one of us thanks our gods by acknowledging their existence in our hearts.

## APPLES AND ORANGES

In the final scene of *My Big Fat Greek Wedding*—a film that's all about finding common ground in disparate cultures—the father of the bride, Gus, makes a funny yet insightful comment during the wedding toast. He says the name Miller, his daughter's new last name, comes from the Greek word for apple, *milo*. Portokalos, Gus' last name, means orange. Finally resigned to the fact that his daughter will marry a non-Greek, he concludes that, despite their cultural differences, "In the end, we're all fruits."

Despite worshipping different religions, we see that Zoey and her friends, Grandma Redbird, and the Benedictine nuns all pray for the same things: guidance, strength, and help. Does it matter, in the end, to which divine female—or even divine male—the prayer goes? Our wishes are born in our hearts and they travel out into the greater universe. Ultimately, our hope is that the universe will catch our need and turn our wish into reality. To help our wishes make their journey safely and give weight to our intentions, we might light a candle or blow one out. Maybe we'll say a prayer, or build an altar. The wishes themselves remain the same.

It's up to each of us to remember that, and to remember that we all reflect a sacred light. Like the Goddess, we have a vast ability for compassion and empathy. We understand that we can be *Tempted*, or lead others astray. Sometimes we hurt others; other times we are *Betrayed*. But at the end of the road, with the right spiritual guidance, we can be *Awakened*. In worshipping our goddesses, we worship ourselves. And I now realize that every time P.C. addressed me as "Goddess Editor" it was her way of saying, as they do in the Hindu tradition, *Namaste*—The divine in me greets the divine in you.

CHRISTINE ZIKA is currently Editor-in-Chief at The Literary Guild and Rhapsody book clubs. She has been an editor for over twenty years and has worked with fiction and nonfiction authors at Avon Books, Dell Publishing, and Berkley Publishing.

# { Cruithne Mythos in the House of Night }

*P.C. Cast*

FIRST, LET me explain why I use the term "Cruithne" and not "Celtic" when I speak of Scottish and Irish Clansfolk.

It may surprise readers to find out that the word most used to describe the culture and people of northwestern Europe, Celtic or Celt, is a modern word that only came into popular usage in the last century. The word comes from a Latin description of a small Spanish tribe that Roman scribes and historians used to create myths about a fictional race they called the Celts. These myths were so successful that, in today's world, it's now generally believed that the Celts were every bit as real as the Romans, when in truth a "Celtic race" only existed in fiction.

The Scots and Irish Gaelic culture we associate with the term today, though, is very real. It just has no connection to those original Roman myths. After the Second World War, with the movement of peoples around Europe, the art and music of the Scots and Irish appealed to the souls of many nations, and they, most specifically of all northwestern Europeans, began to be called Celts.

The Clansfolk of Scotland and Ireland today prefer to be called by their ancient name of Cruithne. Cruithne is a Gaelic word used by Gaels themselves that specifically refers to the indigenous peoples of Scotland, Ireland, and Northwest Wales. This Gaelic word, by definition, incorporates the music, history, myths, legends, gods, and goddesses of the Gaelic peoples (oddly mirroring what the fictional title Celt had been created to do). Why I choose to use Cruithne instead of the more easily recognized Celt is because as I listened to their stories I saw that, in their own language, Cruithne is who they were, are, and ever will be.

WHEN ZOEY'S soul shattered at the end of *Tempted* and I began to research the perfect place to use as a conduit between the modern world and Nyx's Otherworld, Scotland immediately came to mind. I've long felt a connection to Scotland. I've studied Cruithne history and mythology, and as a high school English teacher I led several groups of students to Scotland. I'll always remember the first time I crossed the English/Scottish border in 1994. Our tour bus stopped at one of those huge dividing stones that say "ENGLAND" on one side and "SCOTLAND" on the other. It was raining (of course!), and as I traced my fingers over the damp letters, S C O T L A N D, I thought, *Finally here*. I'd enjoyed England, and still do, but Scotland has had my heart for a long time.

So it felt right for me to look to Scotland for the magick and myth to solve Zoey's Otherworldly dilemma. As I considered the setting, I was drawn to the Scottish Highlands, the Isle of Skye in particular. Some people will call it luck or accident; I like to think of it as listening to and then following my intuition, which was, perhaps, guided by a little nudge from the Goddess. But whatever it was, I found myself in Edinburgh meeting Seoras Wallace, Chieftain of Clan Wallace, who was the research assistant my fabulous UK publisher hired for me. That day in early August of 2009 changed my life, as well as the mythology of the House of Night.

Seoras and I shared an instant connection, and on that sunny August day in the Highlands (yes! The sun does sometimes shine in the Highlands!), I stepped into another world as this Chieftain recognized and honored me as what he called a "shenachie," or a traditional storyteller for the Clan, usually a revered, hereditary position. Seoras introduced me to Clan members who began answering my research questions by sharing with me the gift of their oral history. Because of the respect with which Seoras regarded me, I was accepted by and felt completely at home with his Clan—and not just the men and women in Scotland! Seoras knew I needed more of the ancient Cruithne, so he opened the door to mystical Ireland and one of his Irish Clan brothers. This allowed me to attain a richer, more three-dimensional picture of the Cruithne mythos. In my research for *Burned* I made four lengthy trips to Scotland, and I wove the beautiful Scottish and Irish story threads I discovered there into a new mythological tapestry for the House of Night.

I'd like to share with you a little of the magick I found in Scotland and Ireland, and show you how I absorbed it into Zoey Redbird's world.

*Ireland*

## THE BULLS OF LIGHT AND DARKNESS

My zodiac sign is Taurus; I am truly a bull. So it's not surprising that more than three decades ago when I first discovered that the Scots and Irish had a mythos that centered around two great bulls eternally locked in combat, the stories stuck in my mind.

I'd been thinking about getting a tattoo for years. I mean, obviously I'm interested in them, as they play a major part in the House of Night. But it was in the middle of my second research trip to the Highlands for the House of Night when I came to my first tattoo—literally.

Seoras had been leading me through the Highlands, but when he noticed how interested I was in the old stories of the bulls, he said that I really needed to speak with one of his Irish Clan brothers. Trusting Seoras' intuition completely, I went with him from Glasgow to a little town about an hour and a half outside Dublin, Carraig Mhachaire Rois, where I met Alan Mac au Halpine, a tattoo artist who was more Shaman than modern ink guy (though Alan would not describe himself that way—authentic Shamans rarely do). I talked with him at length about the connection I felt with my earth sign, and he began to speak of the Irish mythology of the bulls. As he told the ancient stories I could finally see my own tattoo: the figure of a bull, the form of a goddess held within the beast.

I asked Alan if he would design the tattoo for me, and all the while he sketched, and then during the three hours he tattooed me, Alan's lilting voice spun stories of bulls and times gone by. It is from Alan's stories that I found a path to create a belief system in the House of Night world that predated Nyx—that was earthy and wild and uncivilized—that represented Light and Darkness in their purest forms.

Perhaps it was the ritualistic, tribal act of the tattoo itself that helped to shape the primeval aspect of the religion I expanded within the House of Night world. Alan did honor me by making the first mark of my tattoo in the ancient way—with a sharpened stick he'd hand-carved, which he dipped in ink and tapped into my flesh. Maybe it was the combination of the pain of the tattoo mixed with the beauty of Alan's artwork, wrapped in the stories he told. Or maybe the sibh (pronounced shee—fairy folk) were drawn to me, a modern shenachie absorbing their ancient homeland stories, and they gathered around the little tattoo shop in the heart of the Irish village so that some of their tales could find their way into the world today, and their magick could touch us all.

Let's see what you think after I share with you a small sample of some of the stories Alan told me that day. Close your eyes, just for a moment. Breathe in deeply. Exhale slowly. Let your imagination take you to verdant Ireland and listen to Alan's lilting voice . . .

*The bulls were the incarnation of two powerful druids; each was a keeper of the spirits of each half of Ireland. They started out as friends, but got into an argument over whose powers were stronger. They fought as different incarnations for hundreds and hundreds of years: first as great eagles, then as great sea monsters, then two great stags, then two war-riors, then two phantoms, then two great dragons. Then, exhausted, they became two maggots.*

*One of the maggots got into the water of Cronn at Cuailinn, where a cow drank it up and gave birth to the Dun Cuailinn, which means the Brown Bull of Cuailinn. This Bull of Cuailinn was dark, dire, haughty with young health. He was horrific, overwhelming, ferocious, full of craft,* with furious, fiery flanks. Brave, brutal, thick-breasted, curly-browed, with a true bull's brow, snorting, mighty in muzzle and eye. He had a royal wrath, and a beast's rage—a bandit's stab, a lion's fury, and a bellow that only the thunder could match. Thirty grown boys could take their place from his rump to his nape. He was a hero and beloved, was the great Brown Bull of Cuailinn.

The other maggot got into the wellspring garden in Connaught and was drunk by another cow. She gave birth to Finn Bennach, the White Bull of the Ai Plain. This bull had a white head, and white hooves, and a red body the color of blood, as if bathed in blood, or dyed in the red bog under his breast and on his back and his heavy mane. With a ponderous tail, and a stallion's breast, and a cow's apple eye, and a salmon snout, and a hind's haunch, he romps in rut. Born to bear victory, bellowing in greatness, his charge is a tempest.

And these two mighty, virile creatures, each representing the spirits of their nation, are still embodying the two druids. Some say until these two druids stop fighting we will never have peace.

So what do you think? Did the sibh touch you, too? Can you see the link between the House of Night's bulls of Light and Darkness, and the Brown Bull of Cuailinn and the White Bull of Ai Plain?

## SEOL NE GIGH[1]—THE SEAT OF THE SPIRIT STONE

The idea to create a huge sacrificial stone with intricate knot work carved all over the sides, down which Stark's blood runs, came from another story Alan told me that day. (Yes, three hours is a long time to get tattooed! Lots of talking and ale-drinking goes on!) This is what Alan told me that inspired the creation of the giant rock that rises from the middle of my fictional House of Night castle on the Isle of Skye:

---

[1] The Gaelic I use is mainly from the Dalriadic and Gallovidian languages from the west coast of Scotland and the northeast coast of Ireland. This dialect is commonly referred to as Gal-Gaelic or GalGael.

*Local legend held that the king who brought the art of gold smelting to Ireland began to worship the blood-hungry god Crom Cruach. Most of this worship centered around sacrifices that took place on what was called either the Plain of Adoration, or the Plain of Decimation, found today in County Cavan, outside the town of Ballyconnell. Crom Cruach's stone wasn't just ornately carved, but was covered in silver. It was said that "the Druids let the blood draw onto the stone, and read the auguries from the flow of blood in the carved channels." Because of the violence of Crom's worshippers, other tribes shunned the area, and didn't marry into them*

There are several versions of what happened to the stone that was at the center of these rituals. One version, Alan told me, is that the stone now dwells in the bowels of the Vatican. Others say it used to be buried, but when in the 1840s locals began leaving flowers and offerings of milk and eggs on the ground above the stone, the Christian church had what they believed to be the stone dug up and smashed. According to this second version, remnants of the stone still "are to be seen in County Cavan to this day."

Then Alan told me a more personal chapter in the story, and it was because of this telling that I was sure that it should be this particular stone, resurrected through my fictionalization, that must serve as the conduit for Stark's painful, near-death quest to the Otherworld.

*Some close friends and I went to find the ancient circle of Crom on a miserable November day, a few years ago. We found the town. It was Sunday, and we didn't see a single soul. We eventually found the old and abandoned stone circle, but a few hundred yards away from it I began to feel giddy and separated myself from the rest of the group. On reaching the circle, I began to feel light-headed and sat down on one of the stones. The inside of my head began to feel squashed, and I became overcome with the need for flight. When I tried to stand up my legs went wobbly, so I sat again. Then I began to feel screaming inside my head rather than hear it, so I tried to centre my thoughts by striking a conversation with the others. But the screaming was now mixed with images that I could not make sense of, so I stood up to walk away, and suddenly began to dry retch. That was enough for me; I will never return. This is the truth as I know it, and as I was told it, and as I pass it to you.*

So it was Alan's soul-felt description that caused me to create a stone that became the Seat of the Spirit of Skye, the perfect conduit through which our Warrior, Stark, held at the brink of death, did what no other living vampyre Warrior had ever before accomplished, and entered the Otherworld!

Do you believe in the sibh now?

## Scotland

Seoras and I only spent a couple of days in Ireland during that trip, because my mind kept circling back to the Highlands and the stories that were calling to me there. I have to admit that my research in Scotland, on the Isle of Skye in particular, was the most satisfying, enjoyable, and productive research trip I've ever taken. Not only did I have a strong, intelligent, knowledgeable Clan Chieftain as my personal guide and research assistant, but through Seoras I met another wonderful historian and Clan member, Alan Torrance,[2] as well as his wife, Denise, who "saved" me from all that Clan Wallace testosterone. She also told her own wonderful stories of the fey, some of which inspired the scenes in *Awakened* where Zoey glimpses the old magick on Skye as it becomes tangible in the forms of elemental fairies. (Honestly, I sometimes think Denise is a little fey herself—she's blonde and beautiful and her cooking is definitely magick!)

Happily, Alan and Denise joined Seoras and me on Skye, and we set out across the island, sloughing through the cold, never-ending rain for several days. And you know what? It was absolutely not as miserable as that just sounded. Not only did we make some fabulous discoveries, like finding the

---

[2] Alan Torrance isn't only a Clan member and a historian, he is also an exceptionally talented artist. It is his work that illustrates this book!

ruins of Sgiach's Castle, discovering ancient groves that seemed part of the Otherworld come to earth, and happening upon the best dang chip shop in the universe, but we also cemented friendships. We returned in the evenings to sit in a warm B&B and tell stories over fabulous food. This Alan, too, shared stories with me that found their way into the House of Night mythos.

## FUNERAL TRADITIONS

Sometimes the smallest details that come to light during research can trigger something that just seems to somehow perfectly fit your needs. That's what happened when Alan told me the story about why there were these strange grooved notches in one of the ruined walls we'd found as we tromped around the Isle of Skye.

The four of us had stopped to rest at an old stone wall that ended up not being far from Sgiach's Castle. I noticed the notches because I was sitting on the wall and I ran my hand over them, thinking aloud that this wall was definitely "broken." Alan smiled and made me study the break in the stones more carefully, and I saw that they were intentional. Then he told me why they were there.

> There was a law brought in at the beginning of the seventeenth century (under King James VI) banning funeral traditions and all they entailed, which often involved transporting bodies over long distances across Scotland, via a stretcher carried by the deceased's closest friends and family. Each took a turn holding part of the stretcher until he or she had to rest, and then they rotated out and another Clan member stepped up and took their place. Obviously the trip would have been difficult because of the rough terrain, especially in the Highlands, so the tribes and Clans developed a system where folk would take the body a certain distance, mostly through their tribal homelands, to an allocated place beside an ancient wall, or dyke, where they could stop and rest. At the time I was finding out about this I was working with Stewart James, a dyker who had worked all over Scotland on these ancient walls. I was sharing with him the information I had been discovering about the funeral parties

*that used to crisscross the land, and how they had partied for days, even weeks. How sometimes old rivalries would arise on the journey or, better than that, sometimes folk would meet and marriages would be created, appeasing Clan disputes. We laughed and lamented that these busy thoroughfares that we found ourselves working on in modern Scotland held such a rich and mostly untold history. It was then Stewart showed me the Through Bands. These are big blocks of stone built through the wall to hold the deceased's litter poles at transfer or even resting points in the journey.*

*The celebration of this tradition by the tribes of ancient Scotland honored the dead in a way that united the Clans, and it was this that most probably intimidated the power-hungry Kings of Scotland and Britain and led to the laws that forbid the practice.*

I was intrigued by the funeral tradition and knew I was going to have to use part of it in the House of Night—and I did! It's a tiny detail, but when Zoey is carried into Sgiach's Castle on a stretcher, she is borne there in this ancient way. To me, this telling added a touch of reverence and authenticity to the scene that set the whole tempo of the rest of the book.

## SGIACH, THE GREAT TAKER OF HEADS

The funeral story was wonderful and it sparked my creativity, but what I needed most was a setting for a House of Night on Skye. Seoras had originally spoken to me of an ancient warrior queen who lived on Skye and who trained the sons and daughters of kings. Alan picked up this tale, describing a woman who lived some time before the sixth century, and this is how I met Sgiach, the Great Taker of Heads.

It was right after Alan first mentioned her that Seoras turned a corner in the small road we were traveling down on Skye. There was a lovely little grove to our left. To our right my eyes were drawn to some highland cows grazing in a boggy field very close to a craggy, rocky coastline. Something caught at my vision and I asked Seoras to stop. We both looked and realized at about the same time that what we were seeing were the ruins of an imposing edifice situated at the top of a sheer cliff overlooking the ocean. We knew it had to be Sgiach's Castle. Later that night back at the B&B we found out we'd been correct, but only after the four of us had spent the day clambering all over the amazing ruin.

Come on! Imagine it with me! It was raining and cold, as I already said, but you need to add wind. Lots of wind, which got crazier and even more blustery after we'd waded through the field and climbed up to the grass and rock mound that was what remained of the great Taker of Heads' Castle.

Alan's art at the beginning of this essay has eerily reconstructed what it could have looked like. That bridgelike entrance he brings alive in the sketch—well, today it has almost no floor. To get to the rest of the castle ruin you have to cross it by scaling the edge on your tiptoes, clutching the crumbly wall and trying not to look down at the more than twenty-foot drop that opens behind and below you.

Well, of course I had to get across it. It was research! Alan went first. Seoras went last, handing Denise and then me off from his strong grip to Alan's before he followed us. Alan was wearing a kilt, and there were what seemed like gale-force gusts whipping *up* from the huge hole where the floor should have been. Do you have a mental picture yet? Let's just say I can report with authority what Scottish men wear under their kilts. In Oklahoma we call it "a whole lot of nuthin'," which is yet another little research tidbit I added to *Burned*.

So after Denise and I stopped giggling like preteens, we all explored the ruins of Sgiach's mighty fortress. The sky was like slate. The wind made my eyes tear. It was even hard to stand sometimes because of the force of it, and it was *freezing*! I began to wonder why the hell anyone would live up here, and then Seoras bumped my shoulder and said, "Look about ye, wumman." It was almost as though Sgiach reached down through the centuries and opened my eyes. From the ruins of her castle I could literally see the vast expanse of the North Atlantic. No one could have snuck up on this queen. Longboats? Viking invasions? Ha! She'd have had her archers in line to kick butt before the enemy could even get close enough to be pummeled on the rocks below. And that's when the character of the Sgiach started to form in my imagination. From walking in her steps I understood the military tactician she must have been, and the wise, protective queen began to emerge.

Though the water at the bottom of the sheer drop was easily more than a hundred feet below us, I swear I could taste the salt in the air, and while I listened to Alan's story it was like Sgiach herself whispered words to me through the Cruithne . . .

I suppose the ultimate honour the people bestowed upon Sgiach was that they named this magnificent island after her. (Or maybe she took her name from it?) As you can see, the landscape of Skye is probably the most jagged in all of Scotland. Its peaks that stab through mists remind me of the qualification required of all students who wanted to learn from Sgiach's school of martial arts. They had to walk barefoot over the two Cuillen mountain ranges before they were considered to be allowed entrance to DunScaichis, or Sgiach's Castle, to become warriors.

My understanding is that the prospective warriors came from all over Europe. Even now in modern Scotland if you are from Skye you are known as a Skianniach. I was speaking with a native Skye woman and asked her about Sgiach and she told me when a young person is called a Sgiach it is often derogatory, a put-down, referring to a troublemaker, a rouge!

A conversation I had recently with another native Skye man who grew up in and around DunScaichis told me of his memories of climbing and camping around Sgiach's Castle. He called it "an intimidating place," and said "bad things have happened there." This may have something to do with the rumor from which she got her name "The Head Taker"; she chopped off the heads of her enemies.

Irish monks who came over to Scotland in the sixth and seventh centuries documented details of how the natives were expected to start training to be warriors at the age of eleven and continued until the age of eighteen. This applied to both young men and women. The monks were obviously intimidated by this tradition, so they proposed a law banning women from taking part in the process to become a warrior, but even up and through many of our battle stories following that time, women played major roles on and off the field. Within the Clan the Warrior Women of Scotland are still respected and loved in modern society.

Alan Torrance's stories, Seoras' guidance, and the physical act of touching, smelling, *knowing* the magnificent setting that was once home to this mighty queen enabled me to bring her alive again through my fictional world. I hope, somewhere, somehow, that makes her smile.

## CLAN MACUALLIS AND THE GUARDIAN MYTHOS

By concluding my essay with Seoras Wallace's interview, I've saved the best for last. I readily admit that I borrowed heavily from Seoras and the history of his Clan in creating the Guardian Mythology and my fictional Clan MacUallis (which is a loose Gaelic translation of Wallace). Seoras told me fascinating stories that had been passed down through his family for centuries, and (with his permission) I absorbed the folk history of Clan Wallace into the House of Night.

Okay, that sounds easy: I just take what a guy tells me and turn it into my own fiction. Uh, not so. Especially not so if the "guy" and his Clan consider you their shenachie. I want to do Clan Wallace proud, and I'd never been so nervous in my professional life as the day Seoras read the manuscript of *Burned*, the book in which the Wallace history first began to weave into the House of Night world. Let me be very clear: I've fictionalized the history of Clan Wallace. I've worked my version of it into the mythology of the House of Night world, just as I've worked Cherokee tradition into that world. Neither are meant to be accurate representations of *actual* history. I do hope that through my creation of the House of Night mythos I have demonstrated the respect and love I feel for both cultures—my greatest desire is for my storytelling to reflect that.

I was intrigued about the respect Clan Wallace showed and still shows women, and I asked Seoras to expand on the historical significance of the idea that their Clan protected Scotland's Ace. I think readers can easily recognize how I incorporated his words into the world of the House of Night through my creation of the Warrior Guardians. And, yes, the fictional Seoras is definitely based on the real man, who Kristin, like Aphrodite, affectionately calls The Shawnus. I also admit that there are definite similarities between my fictional Sgiach and me, especially as I describe the bond between the Queen and her Guardian. It may be indulgent, but I like to believe adding pieces of my real world to my fictional world makes for a more authentic story. It certainly makes it more fun to write!

Here is Seoras' story:

> *The Wallace, Wall-ace, were part of the race of people inhabiting Scotland's Midwest coastlands at the sea mouth of the Clyde (Alcluid). They were known as the Strathclyde Britons, whose central castle/fortification was DunBriton (today known as Dumbarton). The King was known as the Ard Righ, or High King: full title Artur ard Righ. Artur (from Arturus) means the Bear. His queen was titled Bann Righ, or the Ace.*
>
> *The Artur ard Righ sent to all the Clans for their best warriors, male and female, a gathering of the finest of the nation's dedicated warrior class. They put their lives before any threat to the Ace, Bann Righ, who represented all that was precious to the peoples of Strathclyde and guarded the iconic symbols and religions of the race at all costs against Roman, Saxon, or any other enemy.*
>
> *An Ace primarily is represented in the living body of the ancient nation's Queen, who was also of warrior stock and traditionally a trainer of the young blood, or future kings and queens. But the word ace also refers to the iconic symbols of the race. The Guardians carried these totemic symbols to war, and so were the heart of the people. When not at war, these aces were placed originally at the foot of the Antonius wall by the Guardians, who derived their clan name, Wallace, from this action: Wall/Ace.*

This brings me to the role of women in the Clan, both ancient and modern. It's funny that outsiders see only the surface: big, strong, kinda dodgy-looking men who seem invulnerable and anything but matriarchal. The truth is far from it. A true Clan warrior reveres and respects his woman, and the Clan women, with his heart and soul and body. Here's how Seoras describes it:

> *The status of women among the Clan, both ancient and modern, has its basis in the powerful obligation we feel to protect and serve that begins as a boy and then develops into the soul of a man. A woman is worldly stability and procreation of the race. She is recognized in spirit. Her*

*intellect is given equal merit and standing in our society, as can be seen in the genealogy of the Scots in particular. They're known as a small but ferocious race of men but in actuality serve a matriarchal belief system. Simply put, your father may be in question, but you would always know your mother.*

## THE HANGING TREE

The romantic subject of Scottish Clansmen respecting their women is a lovely lead-in to my very favorite research tidbit from the Isle of Skye: the hanging tree.

On this cold, rainy day, Seoras and I were driving around Skye on our own, and we discovered an amazing grove, which I completely re-created for Nyx's Otherworld and used as a temporary haven for Zoey, Heath, and Stark in *Burned*. But what drew our attention to the grove was the tree that stood like a beacon before it. Once again, in the House of Night world, fiction closely mirrors real life. When I describe the hanging tree in the House of Night I am describing this very tree on the Isle of Skye.

Seoras stopped his vehicle and pointed at the tree, which was a hawthorn and a rowan wrapped together. He said, "Aye, that would make a fine hangin' tree."

Okay, as an American I gave him a horrified look. A hanging tree? In front of a serene, mystical grove? How awful! He was quick to see that we'd had a cultural communication error, so he went on to explain:

*Hanging trees are trees of special significance to Scottish Clan folks. A hanging tree is usually of hawthorn, elm, or oak but can be any long-lived tree where Clan folks of the auld religions would hang a piece of material or object, and sometimes even food for the sibh (fairy folk), and simply make a wish, with sincerity, in the hope that wish may come true, also knowing that the wish in its least effect is blessing someone with good health or fortune. A wish is never wasted. Generally it would be for the wellbeing of family or others. Sometimes folk would hang bandages to foster the help of the little people to remedy an injury or illness. Some would hang baby clothes, hoping for pregnancy.*

*The most famous hanging trees in Scotland are at the Black Isle across from Culloden Moor near Inverness. These are reckoned to be hundreds of years old. Many are near springs or running water to invoke the water spirits. Some are near burial grounds where the energies and juices of the burials were taken into the tree for nourishment. Hence the habit of touching wood for luck: if you touch a tree near where a friend or ancestor is buried, you touch the part of that person that is still there in spirit.*

*Another use for the hanging tree was to symbolize the union of "marriage" between two people. They both would take a strip of cloth and then tie a knot, binding the two of them together, safe in the knowledge that only they can untie the knot. The only known Clan to practice this ancient tradition today is the Clan Wallace. For the past twenty years we have inaugurated trees from Shehallion in the center of Scotland to those on the by-ways of all four corners of the land. So, in Scotland, you will always be close to a wishing or hanging tree, if you look for them.*

And I promise you, House of Night fans, if you go to the Isle of Skye and follow a one-lane road where, on your left, a grove stretches down a sloping ridge like the back of a sleeping dragon, you will see at its head a tree, hawthorn and rowan joined, that is decorated by strips of cream and gold cloth from an American author tied with the earthen-tone plaid of a Scottish Clan Chieftain, binding the two of us together. If you find it, friends, please stop and add your own wishes, dreams, and fondest desires to the tree. It will welcome you, just as I welcome you to the rich and varied history that has become the Cruithne tied lovingly with the House of Night.

Merry meet, merry part, and merry meet again . . .

# { Behind the House of Night Names }

What's in a name? Well, after reading how P.C. Cast discovered and wove the Cruithne myths into her tales, you now know that much time and research has gone into creating the intricate plotlines of the House of Night novels. The same is true for the names of the characters.

Below is an appendix of the more intriguing names in the series. You won't find everyone's here; with some names, like Heath Luck or Erik Night, what you see is what you get. But for others, we've untangled the historical, mythological, and pop culture ties—inwtentional and incidental—that give these characters' monikers a little extra magic.

( 

## THE FLEDGLINGS

### Zoey Redbird

*Zoey (Greek)* life; *Redbird* in Cherokee myth, the Redbird is the daughter of the Sun

*In the House of Night . . .*

During their first meeting in *Marked*, Nyx calls Zoey *u-s-ti Do-tsu-wa*, or "little Redbird." Redbird is also the last name of Zoey's grandmother Sylvia, and when Zoey enters the House of Night, she takes this name as her own.

*In mythology . . .*

Jealous that the people of Earth could look upon her brother the Moon without squinting, the Sun sent down a vicious heat wave to kill them. To stop her, the people sent two snakes to attack the Sun during her daily visit to her daughter's house in the middle of the sky. The copperhead snake failed, but the rattlesnake, overly eager to complete the task, accidently struck the Sun's daughter and killed her. Grieved, the Sun left the world to mourn, plunging everything into darkness. Seven men were sent to the Ghost World to retrieve Redbird's spirit, put her in a box, and bring her home without opening it. But near the end, they cracked the lid to make sure she hadn't smothered, and a redbird flew out and away.

*Of note . . .*

Ironically enough, given that Zoey is a vampyre, this myth is meant to explain why people cannot be brought back from the dead. That is, of course, not the only irony here: though Zoey is a daughter of Nyx, the Goddess of Night, she is named after the daughter of the sun.

# Aphrodite
### (*Greek*) risen from the sea

*In mythology . . .*

Aphrodite is the Greek goddess of beauty, love, and sexuality. Her name is taken from the Greek word *aphros* (sea foam) and refers to her birth: she rose from the sea where the castrated member of Ouranos (the sky and father of the gods) was tossed.

*In the House of Night . . .*

By far the prickliest of Zoey's circle, Aphrodite shares common traits with her namesake. Both are extraordinary beautiful and known to exhibit ferocious pride, haughtiness, and jealousy when they feel their status is threatened by another woman.

*Of note . . .*

When Aphrodite's roommate first came to the House of Night she took the name Venus, the Roman version of the goddess Aphrodite.

# Damien
### (*Greek*) to tame

*In the House of Night . . .*

Damien is the studious one in Zoey's circle. He is often the most levelheaded and objective—dare we say tamest?—of the bunch.

*In reality . . .*

Damien is based on P.C.'s former student and research assistant, John Maslin, who found the quote from Hesiod about Nyx and the House of Night that begins *Marked*, the first book in the series. As fledglings who are Marked get to choose their own name, P.C. offered John the same opportunity. Thus we have Damien, a fledgling with an affinity for air and research.

# Erin

*(Irish)* derived from *Éirinn*, meaning "Ireland"

*In the House of Night . . .*
Erin is the blonde half of the infamous Twins and has an affinity for water.

*Of note . . .*
Given Erin's affinity for water and the Irish and Cruithne elements that appear in the later books in the series, it seems appropriate that she shares a name with one of the largest islands in the world.

# Deino, Enyo, Pemphredo

*(Greek)* Deino (terrible), Enyo (warlike), Pemphredo (wasp)

*In mythology . . .*
In Greek myth, the Graiai or "Gray Sisters" are sea-daimons and sisters to the Gorgons (of which Medusa is probably the most famous). Either two or three in number, depending on the myth, the Graiai are said to share one eye and one tooth among them. By stealing their eye, the hero Perseus was able to find the three objects needed to kill Medusa.

*In the House of Night . . .*
Deino, Enyo, and Pemphredo are the three fledglings who make up Aphrodite's inner circle of friends in *Marked*. They are unaffectionately labeled "the Hags from Hell" by Erin and Shaunee.

# James Stark

*James Stark* taken from the character Jim Stark, James Dean's character
in *Rebel Without a Cause*

*In the movie . . .*
*Rebel Without a Cause* has become a cult classic for generations of "misunderstood teenagers" and James Dean in that red windbreaker the symbol of living fast and dying young.

*In the House of Night . . .*
It's unclear if James Stark also took his first name from James Dean, but it

is certain from the moment he is introduced in *Untamed* that he is a bit of a rebel. Incidentally, the archer also "dies" very young. (Luckily, he is resurrected and eventually finds his way back to the Light in *Hunted*.) Stark's original surname was MacUallis, which marked him as one of the Guardians of the Ace (see *Seoras*).

*Of note . . .*
Red windbreaker, red vampyre. Coincidence? We'll leave that up to you

# Jack Twist

*Jack Twist taken from the character Jack Twist in* Brokeback Mountain

*In the movie . . .*
*Brokeback Mountain* is the story of two cowboys who fall in love and must keep their relationship hidden, mostly through the means of unhappy marriages. Jack Twist is by far the more outgoing and passionate half of the couple. This may or may not have contributed to his death, which was either from changing a tire that exploded or his being beaten to death after his sexuality was discovered.

*In the House of Night . . .*
Jack Twist is the bubbliest of Zoey's circle, sensitive and innocent almost to the point of being childlike, and like his namesake, he is the dramatic half of his relationship with Damien.

# Shaunee

*Shaunee taken from the Shawnee Indian tribe, also the
town of Shawnee, Oklahoma*

*In history . . .*
The Shawnee Indians were only one of many tribes that settled around what is now known as Shawnee, Oklahoma, after the Civil War. All three federally recognized Shawnee tribes are based in Oklahoma today: the Absentee-Shawnee Tribe in Shawnee, the Eastern Shawnee Tribe in West Seneca, and the Shawnee Tribe in Miami.

*In the House of Night . . .*
Shaunee is the brunette half of the Twins. She has an affinity for fire that matches her sometimes fierce temper. Despite her name's Oklahoma connections, she hails from Connecticut.

(

## THE VAMPYRES

· · ·

### HOUSE OF NIGHT PROFESSORS

## Anastasia Lankford

*Anastasia (Greek)* resurrection; *Lankford* see *Dragon Lankford*

*In Christianity . . .*

Anastasia of Sirmium was a Christian saint and martyr. She is specially com-
memorated in the second Mass on Christmas day. Not much is known about
her actual life, and legends conflict as to whether she was Roman or not and
even who she was exactly. However, it is certain that Anastasia gave her life
for her faith in Sirmium, and because of this her memory was kept sacred. St.
Anastasia is also revered as a healer. The Eastern Orthodox Church calls her
"Deliverer from Potions" and she is often called upon to protect people from
poison and harmful substances.

*In the House of Night . . .*

Anastasia was married to Professor Dragon Lankford. She taught Rituals and
Spells at the Tulsa House of Night, and she was among the few professors who
fought against the Raven Mockers in *Hunted*. Anastasia was also the single
casualty of that fight. Murdered by Rephaim, her sacrifice helped allow Zoey
and her friends to safely escape the overrun campus.

*In reality . . .*

The real Anastasia Lankford is married to Bryan Lankford, the inspiration for
the character Dragon Lankford.

## Dragon Lankford

*Dragon (Greek)* derived from *drakōn*, a large serpent, python, or dragon;
*Lankford* taken from Bryan Lankford, on whom the character is based

*In mythology . . .*

Dragons of Eastern myth are benevolent, often bringing good fortune and symbolizing excellence and power. However, dragons of European myth are often evil. They are intelligent, but extremely greedy and selfish.

*In the House of Night . . .*

Dragon Lankford is the fencing instructor at the House of Night. His facial tattoos are in the form of two dragons breathing fire at the crescent symbol in the middle of his forehead.

*In reality . . .*

Dragon Lankford's real-life counterpart, Bryan Lankford, who wrote an essay for this book, is also an educator: he writes books and leads classes on Wicca. After winning the chance to become a new character in the House of Night series in a charity auction at an autumn Pagan gathering where P.C. was speaking, Bryan and his wife, Anastasia, were added to the cast of vampyres.

*Of note . . .*

Dragon Lankford's name also evokes the story of the red dragon in Welsh myth and Arthurian legend. The red dragon was said to be a prophecy of the coming of King Arthur, famous puller of the sword from the stone. Arthur's father was named Uther Pendragon, "chief dragon" or "dragon's head." And how about this for a cool coincidence: Anastasia Lankford's cat shares a name with Guinevere, King Arthur's queen. (Although given that P.C. is of Welsh descent, maybe there's more to this than coincidence after all . . .)

## Lenobia

*Lenobia* taken from Zenobia, queen of the empire of Palmyrene

*In history . . .*

After her husband and his eldest successor were assassinated, Zenobia became regent for her one-year-old son in A.D. 267, ruling the Roman colony of Palmyrene in present-day Syria. In her new position, Zenobia swiftly conquered Egypt in 269 and declared Palmyrene independent from Rome. The Warrior Queen, as she came to be called, would conquer much of Asia Minor before her defeat and capture by the emperor Aurelian. There are many stories of how her life ended, but the most common is that Aurelian, impressed by her courage and audacity, freed Zenobia and granted her clemency. She was said to have married a Roman senator and lived the remainder of her life peacefully in a villa in Tibur, modern-day Tivoli, Italy.

*In the House of Night . . .*

Lenobia's tattoos consist of intricate knots in the shape of two rearing horses, fitting for the equestrian professor!

*Of note . . .*

Among her many attributes, Queen Zenobia was especially admired for her skill in horseback riding, a rare accomplishment for a woman in third-century Syria.

## Loren Blake

*Loren (Latin)* the short form of the name Lawrence,
meaning "from Laurentum," an ancient Roman city; *Blake* taken from the
English poet William Blake

*In history . . .*

The city of Laurentum took its name from *laurus*, the Latin word for laurels. In ancient times, poets, heroes, and winners of athletic contests (laureates) were crowned with wreaths of laurels as a mark of honor.

*In history, take two . . .*

William Blake was a painter and a printmaker, but he is probably best known today as one of the prominent poets of the Romantic period (unfortunately he wasn't appreciated much until *after* his death in 1827). From the age of four, Blake, a nonconformist with great respect for the creative imagination, claimed to have heavenly visions. When his brother Robert died from consumption, Blake claimed he saw Robert's spirit fly from his body, clapping in joy. Robert's spirit would visit Blake from time to time and even told him about a special printing method. Blake's artwork was also highly revered, and he was commissioned to do the drawings for a version of Dante's *Divine Comedy*.

*In the House of Night . . .*

Before his death in *Betrayed*, Loren Blake was the vampyre poet laureate. Though we never see him recite one of his own poems, we do see Loren draw inspiration from Shakespeare (a vampyre poet in the series) and Japanese haiku.

## Neferet

*(Egyptian)* beautiful woman

*In history . . .*

Neferet from the House of Night might loosely borrow her name, and her ego, from Queen Nefertiti. While her husband remains obscure (what was his name again . . . right, Akhenaten!), Nefertiti is probably the most famous of the ancient Egyptian Queens after Cleopatra. Not only was she beautiful, history suggests she wielded quite a bit of power. She helped Akhenaten begin a radical religious revolution, monotheism, in which only Aten, the disk of the sun, was worshipped.

*In the House of Night . . .*

Neferet is as beautiful as she is dangerous and intelligent, and she uses her beauty and power to captivate those around her and hide her darkness. If beauty is a weapon, the Queen Tsi Sgili is an assassin who proves time after time in the series that she cannot be controlled by anyone, much less her unawares Akehenaten, Kalona.

*Of note . . .*

As the royal power couple and "gods upon earth," Egyptians were expected to worship Aten by worshipping Nefertiti and Akhenaten. Nefertiti even changed her name to Neferneferuaten-Nefertiti, meaning "The Aten is radiant [because] the beautiful one has come." See any similarities to the Neferet/Nyx, Kalona/Erebus switcheroo?

## Penthesilea

*(Greek)* mourned by the people; mournful grip

*In mythology . . .*

The Amazon queen Penthesliea led her troops into battle against the Greeks in the Trojan War. She was killed by the warrior Achilles.

*In the House of Night . . .*

Professor Penthesilea, or Professor P as she likes to be called, teaches literature. Zoey remarks that she looks like something out of a sci-fi film, with long red-blonde hair and thin Celtic knot Marks that make her face look dramatic. The vampyre Amazon queen Penthesilea is the first historical figure Zoey learns about at the House of Night in her Vampyre Sociology class with Neferet.

*Of note . . .*

Another great Amazon queen's story, that of Hippolyte and her imprint with the Greek hero Herakles, can be found in *The Fledgling Handbook 101*.

# Sappho

(*Greek*) taken from the seventh-century poet Sappho of the island of Lesbos

*In history . . .*

Sappho is well known for her writings on the hidden lives of women. She also wrote about love between women, and it is her name from which the term "Sapphic" originates.

*In the House of Night . . .*

The media librarian at the House of Night is named Sappho. The historical Sappho is portrayed as a vampyre poet.

# Vento

(*Italian*) wind

*In a word . . .*

The surname *Vento* may have derived from *aventure*, a bold or adventurous person. It is also the short form of the name *Bonaventura*, or "good fortune."

*In the House of Night . . .*

Professor Vento sided with Neferet and Kalona during the takeover of the House of Night school. (It's possible her allegiance can be swayed any way the wind blows.)

*In reality . . .*

Professor Vento is based on a real person, Steve Vento, a teacher and band director at South Intermediate High School in Tulsa (the basis for Zoey's former high school).

* * *

## THE SONS OF EREBUS

# Darius

(*Persian/Greek*) 1. To possess; rich, kingly 2. Upholder of the good

*In history . . .*

Darius was a popular name among ancient Persian kings, but the most well known was Darius the Great, who conquered parts of Greece to greatly expand the Persian empire. He organized a new monetary system and declared Aramaic the official language. In addition to numerous building projects, he left behind his autobiography, the Behistun Inscription, carved onto the face a cliff.

*In the House of Night . . .*

Darius is Aphrodite's sworn warrior and consort. He was gifted with super speed by Nyx, and though he is a young vampyre, he demonstrates vast knowledge and skills that have kept Zoey and her circle alive from book to book. Clearly, he's a warrior who upholds the good!

# Aristos

*(Greek)* excellence

*In a word . . .*

The root word *aristo* can also be found in the word aristocracy, a governing body comprised of the most qualified individuals or nobility in a society.

*In the House of Night . . .*

Aristos is a warrior of the Sons of Erebus, whose gifted male vampyres are known for their excellence in battle and their fierce protection of their priestesses.

# Ate

*(Greek)* taken from the Greek goddess Ate

*In myth . . .*

The daughter of Eris (Strife/Discord), Ate was the personification of ruin, rash foolishness of blind impulse, and delusion.

*In literature . . .*

P.C., who taught William Shakespeare's *Julius Caesar* for over a decade, took the name Ate from one of her favorite parts of the play, Mark Antony's soliloquy over Caesar's body: "And Caesar's spirit, raging for revenge, with Ate by his side come hot from hell, shall in these confines with a monarch's voice cry 'Havoc!' and let slip the dogs of war, that this foul deed shall smell above the earth with carrion men, groaning for burial."

*In the House of Night . . .*

Ate was the leader of the Sons of Erebus. He was killed while coming to the defense of Shekinah in *Untamed*. Though his actions during the rise of Kalona did not mirror that of his goddess namesake, the actions of the House of Night vampyres following his death, especially their acceptance of Kalona as Erebus and Neferet as Nyx, truly followed the spirit of the goddess of delusion and blind impulse. And, much like what happened to Brutus and the other Roman conspirators after their rash murder of Caesar, this acceptance swiftly leads the House of Night to dark ruin and tragedy in *Hunted*.

. . .

## THE VAMPYRE HIGH COUNCIL

## Aether
*(Greek)* pure fresh air; clear sky

*In mythology . . .*

Aether, the son of Nyx and Erebus, is the first of the elemental gods in Greek myth. He is the personification of the heavens and the upper regions of space.

*In the House of Night . . .*

Though her namesake is male, Aether is a woman, and a member of the vampyre high council.

## Shekinah
*(Hebrew)* the glorious presence or manifestation of God
dwelling among men

*In mythology . . .*

In Judaism, the Shekinah sometimes refers to the feminine aspects of God. As such, some scholars of the Kabbalah link the Shekinah to the Divine Feminine. In Rabbinic literature, the Shekinah is the actual presence of God come to Earth; God's presence was said to manifest on earth during acts of personal need, public prayer, and righteous judgment. The Shekinah has taken on many forms, including a beam of light, the burning bush through which God (or Yahweh) spoke to Moses, and a cloud leading Israel out of Egypt. The Christian equivalent of the Shekinah in the New Testament is the Holy Spirit, which is often represented in scripture as a dove, light, fire, cloud, and water. As a part of the Holy Trinity, the Holy Spirit is one of the beings that constitutes God, but is also a separate entity sent down to earth to show God's physical presence and carry out the Lord's will. According to the New Testament, Jesus was conceived via the Holy Spirit, who also made an appearance at his baptism, and after his death the Spirit came to Jesus' apostles in tongues of flame that graced them with the power to speak all the world's languages.

*In the House of Night. . .*

Shekinah is the High Priestess of all vampyres. She is very closely allied with Nyx, and Zoey automatically detects the Goddess' presence in the High Priestess when they first meet. As the Hebrew roots of her name imply, Shekinah is regarded by other vampyres as Nyx's presence manifested on earth.

## Thanatos
### *(Greek)* death

*In mythology . . .*

Thanatos is the son of Nyx and the god of nonviolent death.

*In the House of Night . . .*

Thanatos is the only vampyre with an affinity for death. She can talk to and help souls as they cross over to the Otherworld, aligning her conceptually with mythic figures Erebus (see *Erebus*) and Charon (ferryman of the river Styx, who some myths say was one of Nyx's children).

• • •

## THE CRUITHNE

## Sgiach
### *Sgathaich (Gaelic)* shadowy; the shadowed one

*In history . . .*

Sgathaich, "the Great Taker of Heads," was a Scottish warrior queen who ran a military school on the south end of the Isle of Skye (the land of shadows). Her stronghold was Dun Sgathaich, or Dunscaith Castle. Heroes of Scottish legend were said to have gone to "the Fortress of Shadows" to learn the art of warfare.

*In the House of Night . . .*

Like her historical namesake, the vampyre warrior queen Sgiach runs a warrior House of Night school on the Isle of Skye (also known in the books as the Isle of Women). She, too, is called "the Great Taker of Heads," and she has an affinity for the island. As such, she can appear and disappear anywhere on it at will, much like the shadows the real Isle of Skye are associated with.

## Seoras MacUallis

*Seoras (Gaelic)* farmer; the Scottish form of George
*MacUallis (Scottish)* a loosely translated Scottish version of the
last name Wallace

*In reality . . .*

P.C. based this character off the Scotsman Seoras Wallace, the Chieftain of Clan Wallace and the guide hired by her UK publisher when she traveled to Scotland to research *Burned*. He is a descendant of Scottish resistance hero William Wallace and also a sword master and fight director.

*In the House of Night . . .*

Seoras MacUallis is the warrior and defender of Sgiach. He is also James Stark's ancestor and the head of the Clan MacUallis, Guardians of the Ace.

## GODS AND HUMANS

# Nyx
### (Greek) night

*In mythology . . .*

Born from Chaos, Nyx is the primordial goddess of the night. Aether (upper air/atmosphere) and Hemera (day) are her children with Erebus, her consort and brother. Independently, Nyx gave birth to a number of deities, among them the Fates, Eris, and the Hesperides, the female guards of the tree with the golden apples.

*In the House of Night . . .*

Though she is the personification of night, Nyx is closely allied with the Black Bull of Light. She is the central goddess in the vampyre religion and embodies the personas of goddesses from various cultures. In *Marked*, Nyx tells Zoey she has been called:

*Changing Woman*: the central goddess of the Navajo religion. She ages with the seasons, representing the cycle of life and fertility. She is a close personification of the earth and also represents the natural order of the universe.

*Gaea/Gaia*: the Greek primordial goddess who is literally the Earth. She was part of the first group of gods who came into existence independently.

*A'akuluujjusi*: the great creator mother in Inuit religion.

*Kuan Yin*: the goddess of mercy and compassion in Eastern Buddhism. She is highly venerated for her humanity across Asia, especially in China, and it is believed that when a Buddhist dies, Kuan Yin will put their soul in a lotus flower and then send them onto paradise.

*Grandmother Spider*: a creator goddess in many Native American religions. She created the world, and in one Cherokee myth, she stole the sun and brought it to the Cherokee people in a large clay pot, also giving them the gifts of fire and pottery.

*Dawn*: Aurora (Latin) or Eos (Greek) was the goddess of the dawn. In Roman mythology, she flew across the sky to announce the coming of the sun. In Greek mythology, she opened the gates of heaven for Apollo so he could drive his sun chariot across the sky.

# A-ya
## (Cherokee) me

*In the House of Night . . .*

A-ya is an original myth created by the Casts for the House of Night series. Sculpted from earth clay, A-ya was created solely for the purposes of trapping Kalona. The Ghigua called her *A-ya*, or me, because she had a piece or trait of each of the wise women placed inside her. Zoey is a reincarnation of A-ya. In *Burned* we learn that A-ya is also the name of the persona of compassion in Zoey's soul.

*Of note . . .*

P.C. chose the name A-ya in part because this figure could embody that something magickal that exists in every woman.

# Brighid
## (Celtic) exalted one

*In mythology . . .*

Brighid is the goddess of the British Isles and the patron of poets, healers, artisans, inspiration, and fertility. She is also the goddess of fire and hearth. St. Brigid of Kildare, one of Ireland's patron saints, is closely associated with the Pagan goddess. St. Brigid's cross resembles a Pagan sun wheel, and it is often hung in kitchens to protect homes from fire and evil.

*In the House of Night . . .*

In *Burned*, Brighid appears to Zoey in the Otherworld as a tall goddess-like woman with bright, fiery red hair. She is the strength persona of Zoey's soul.

# Erebus
## (Greek) deep darkness or shadow

*In mythology . . .*

Erebus is the embodiment of primordial darkness. He is described as the region in Hades (the Underworld) where the dead pass immediately after dying. From Erebus, the spirits are ferried across the river Styx by Charon to enter the land of the dead.

*In the House of Night . . .*

Erebus is the namesake of the Sons of Erebus, the male vampyre warriors who protect their society (and Nyx's priestesses) fiercely (see *Darius*).

# Kalona

*(Cherokee)* taken from the *Kalona Ayeliski,* or "Raven Mockers,"
also referred to as angels of death

*In mythology . . .*

The worst of the Cherokee witches, the Raven Mockers of Cherokee myth steal the hearts of the old and sick in order to add on to their own life spans, and these thefts contribute to their old and withered appearance. Raven Mockers can be male or female. As a Raven Mocker dives to collect the sick and dying it croaks like a raven, explaining the creature's name and alerting all that death has come.

*In the House of Night . . .*

After being tossed from the Otherworld by Nyx for loving her too much, Kalona fell to earth. He became a god among the Cherokee and was good until he succumbed to his dangerous lust for the women of the tribe. Kalona, who had wings the color of night, could also change into an animal that looked like an enormous raven; thus, the women he raped gave birth to Raven Mockers. After being trapped in the earth for centuries by A-ya, Kalona is resurrected by Neferet and the blood of Stevie Rae, whose affinity for earth releases him from his underground prison. No longer obsessed with stalking Cherokee maidens, he sets his sights on one in particular, Zoey, the reincarnation of A-ya and the being on earth closest to his former Goddess, Nyx.

*Of note . . .*

Kalona was created by the Casts to explain the origins of the Raven Mockers in the House of Night; he does not exist within actual Cherokee myth. Sylvia Redbird compares him to the Nephilim (a biblical race of half-angel supermen who survived the flood of Noah) and to the Greek and Roman Olympian gods. Both Kalona and his son Rephaim were inspired by the Christian myth of Lucifer, the "light-bearer" or "Morning Star." Like Kalona, the former arch-angel was cast down from heaven after attempting to elevate his power to that of God. According to biblical stories, after his fall Lucifer, who is also called Satan, refocused his attentions on humanity, leading God's followers astray and building an army for the time when he would attempt to overthrow his former master and take his place in heaven.

## Rephaim

*(Hebrew)* 1. Shade or spirit (from the netherworld) 2. To heal

*In mythology . . .*

The term Rephaim refers to two separate things in Hebrew mythology. The first is a biblical race of giants closely related to the Nephilim (Goliath was said to be a Rephaim). Rephaim also refers to shades or spirits from the netherworld. Etymologically, the word Rephaim derives from the Hebrew verb meaning, "to heal."

*In the House of Night . . .*

Rephaim is the firstborn and favorite of Kalona's Raven Mocker children. The Hebrew spirit/shade meaning of his name is linked to the Cherokee *Kalona Ayeliski*, as Rephaim embodies all of these myths and implications. Like the biblical Rephaim, he is a mixture of the divine and human. As a *Kalona Ayeliski*, he is a creature of darkness and life-stealing shade (he kills Anastasia Lankford in *Hunted*). But most notably in the House of Night series, he is a source of strength and of healing for Stevie Rae. He saves her from death on two occasions and heals her rapidly with his blood.

## Sylvia Redbird

*Sylvia (Latin)* from the forest; *Redbird (See Zoey Redbird)*

*In mythology . . .*

In Roman mythology, Rhea Silvia is the mother of Romulus and Remus, mythic twins who were nurtured by a she-wolf and founded the city of Rome.

*In the House of Night . . .*

Zoey's grandmother and a wise Cherokee Ghigua, Sylvia is Zoey's link to her Cherokee heritage. As Zoey's relationship with her mother is shaky at best, it is Sylvia who nurtures Zoey during her rebirth and trials at the House of Night. She taught Zoey about the herbs and plants that Zoey incorporates into many of the vampyre rituals in the series.

☾

## THE FAMILIARS

## Beelzebub
### (*Hebrew*) lord of the flies

*In mythology* . . .
Beelzebub is probably a corruption of *Ba'al Zəbûl*, which refers to the ancient god Ba'al and means "Lord of the High Place." In John Milton's *Paradise Lost*, Beelzebub is Satan's lieutenant.

*In the House of Night* . . .
The Beelzebub of the House of Night is a cat—Shaunee and Erin's, specifically. While he isn't evil, he's definitely got some attitude (like his owners!).

## Cameron
### (*Scottish*) crooked nose

*In history* . . .
Cameron is the name of a Scottish clan (Clan Cameron).

*In the House of Night* . . .
Cameron is Damien's cat.

*In reality* . . .
Cameron is the cat version of P.C.'s Wheaton Scottie dog, Cameron.

## Duchess
### *Duchess* title of nobility within a monarchy

*In history* . . .
Traditionally, the title of Duke was the highest in the nobility after the monarchy. A duchess could be the wife of the Duke, or she could hold the title in her own right. The current Queen Elizabeth II is also known as the Duke of Normandy.

*In the House of Night* . . .
The only canine familiar in the series, Duchess is initially James Stark's dog, but her ownership is later shared with Jack Twist.

*Of note . . .*

Duchess' name is the Casts' nod to John Wayne, who as a child had a big dog named Duke. (This is actually the origin of the actor's nickname, "the Duke.")

## Guinevere

*(Welsh)* fair and white, smooth

*In mythology . . .*

Queen Guinevere was the wife of King Arthur and the lover of Sir Lancelot. Her affair with the knight is said to have brought down Camelot and the Knights of the Round Table. Her name is most likely Welsh, the basic meaning being "Gwenhwy the Great."

*In the House of Night . . .*

Guinevere is Anastasia Lankford's cat. Thankfully, in the series she does not bring about misery for Dragon Lankford (that blame belongs to Rephaim).

## Maleficent

*Maleficent* taken from the character of the evil queen in *Sleeping Beauty*

*In the movie . . .*

The prefix *mal* means wrong, ill, or improper, and there could be no better prefix for the "Mistress of All Evil." Pissed that she wasn't invited to Princess Aurora's christening party with the other fairies, Maleficent curses the infant to prick her finger on a spindle and die on her sixteenth birthday. At Disney's Villains Victory Party in October 2010, Maleficent was voted the baddest Disney villain of them all.

*In the House of Night . . .*

Like her owner Aphrodite and her Disney namesake, Maleficent the cat is prone to bouts of bitchiness and violence. She is a white purebred Persian, and has love for no one save her owner.

## Nala

*(Swahili)* gift; taken from the character Nala in *The Lion King*

*In the movie . . .*

Nala is the smart, feisty lioness who finds Simba after he runs away from his lion pride after the death of his father. She gets Simba to return, freeing herself and the rest of the pride from the evil Scar.

*In the House of Night . . .*

Nala first appears to Zoey in a dream. Though she never speaks a word, her general message is "Hurry up and find me, woman!" Eventually, she gets tired of waiting and finds Zoey herself. Like all cats at the House of Night (and Stark and Jack's dog Duchess), Nala is a gift that also has ownership of her fledgling. Her scenes mostly consist of either warning and protecting Zoey—talk about smart and feisty—or sneezing (*mee-uf-ow!*).

*Of note . . .*

Nala is based on a cat Kristin had for years. (She was just like the fictional one, grumpiness, sneezing, and all!)

# Nefertiti
### (*Egyptian*) the beautiful one has arrived (also see *Neferet*)

*In history . . .*

Nefertiti is one of the most well-known queens of ancient Egypt (see *Neferet*).

*In the House of Night . . .*

Nefertiti is Darius' cat. And as the warrior is highly courteous, there is no question he treats this cat like a queen.

*Of note . . .*

Cats were highly esteemed in many parts of ancient Egypt and were even mummified after death (although sometimes as offerings to Bast). The Egyptian pantheon also contained many cat goddesses. So it seems fitting Darius would name his cat after a beautiful queen from this cat-loving nation.

# Persephone
### (*Greek)* daughter of Demeter (goddess of the harvest)
### and Zeus (king of the gods)

*In mythology . . .*

Persephone was minding her own business, planting flowers in her mother's garden one day, when Hades, god of the Underworld, rose up from the earth in a chariot and kidnapped her. Hades was forced to return her after Demeter's grief caused the earth and crops to wither and die, but not before he tricked Persephone into eating some pomegranate seeds. Those who eat food from the land of the dead must return, and thus Persephone would spend part of the year with her mother and part of the year with her husband. During the time she is with Hades, the earth dies again in winter. But when she returns, it reawakens in spring.

*In the House of Night . . .*

Persephone is a mild-mannered horse cared for by Lenobia and the fledglings in the House of Night stables.

*Of note . . .*

Horses appear many times in Greek myth as drawers of the gods' chariots. Nyx is often depicted in a chariot drawn by horses, and we see in *Marked* that Zoey has a natural affinity for them.

# Skylar

*(Dutch)* from the name Schuyler, meaning "scholar"

*In reality . . .*

Skylar was a cat of P.C.'s that has since gone on to frolic with the Goddess. Sky was also labeled as a "known biter" by his vet.

*In the House of Night . . .*

Skylar is Neferet's cat. A bit less feisty than his namesake, he tells Neferet that Nala is on her way to Zoey.

# Shadowfax

*(Old English)* shadow-hair

*In the books . . .*

Shadowfax is Gandalf the Gray's horse in J.R.R. Tolkien's Lord of the Rings books. The silvery-gray stallion can understand human speech and can outrun any horse in Middle-earth. He will wear no bridle or saddle, and only permits Gandalf to ride him.

*In the House of Night . . .*

Shadowfax is Dragon Lankford's cat. Because of their bonds with their owners, Shadowfax and the other House of Night cats can and do communicate with their fledglings/vampyres at an uncanny level. And like Middle-earth's Shadowfax, the cats choose their two-legged partners carefully.

*Of note . . .*

Shadowfax is also based on a real cat owned by P.C.'s friend Christopher Matthews. Shadowfax has moved on to join Skylar with the Goddess.

# { Acknowledgments }

## FROM P.C.

Thank you to Alan Torrance for creating such beautiful art.

A special thank you to Leah Wilson and the BenBella family. It is always such a pleasure to work with you!

## FROM THE PUBLISHER

Thank you to Olubunmi Mia Olufemi for her invaluable work on "Behind the House of Night Names."